Your receipt

Customer ID: **********2696

Items that you checked out

Title:
 The adventures of Grandmaster Flash :
 my life, my beats
ID: 33477456360499
Due: Wednesday, March 27, 2019

Total items: 1
Account balance: $0.00
3/6/2019 4:09 PM
Checked out: 3
Overdue: 0
Hold requests: 0
Ready for pickup: 0

Thank you for using the 3M™ SelfCheck
System.

The Adventures of

GRANDMASTER

The Adventures of

GRANDMASTER

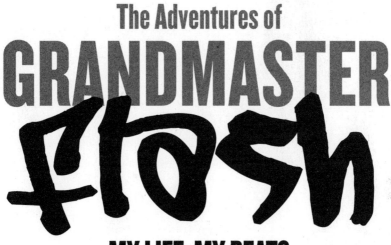

MY LIFE, MY BEATS

Grandmaster Flash
with David Ritz

Broadway Books

New York

BROADWAY

PUBLISHED BY BROADWAY BOOKS

Published in the United States by Broadway Books, an imprint of
The Doubleday Publishing Group, a division of Random House, Inc.,
New York.
www.broadwaybooks.com

BROADWAY BOOKS and its logo, a letter B bisected on the diagonal, are
trademarks of Random House, Inc.

Frontispiece copyright © Charlie Ahearn

Library of Congress Cataloging-in-Publication Data
Grandmaster Flash.
The adventures of Grandmaster Flash : my life, my beats / by
Grandmaster Flash with David Ritz. — 1st ed.
p.   cm.
1. Grandmaster Flash. 2. Rap musicians—United States—Biography.
I. Ritz, David. II. Title.
ML420.G915A3 2008
782.421649092—dc22
[B]
2007048224

ISBN 978-0-7679-2475-7

PRINTED IN THE UNITED STATES OF AMERICA

1   3   5   7   9   10   8   6   4   2

FIRST EDITION

In memory of my parents, Regina "Gina" and
Joseph "Bra" Saddler Sr.

For my sisters—
Penny, Lilly, Violet, and Carmetta;

My children—
Tawanna, Joe Jr., Lalonnie, Kareem, Keith, Christina, and
Christina's big sister Amber;

And the Furious Five—Mel, Cowboy, Kid Creole, Scorpio, and
Rahiem, my love runs deep, even today.

This is a book written by me, Joseph Robert Saddler.

This is a book written by me, Grandmaster Flash.

What's the difference between the two? One name was given to me at birth. The other was invented.

What do these two identities have to do with each other? I'm not sure. That's why I'm writing this book.

It's a small story and a big story.

Small because it's just a story about a guy, like millions of guys, running around trying to play the game. But it's big because, due to forces in the universe—God or fate or whatever—I helped create something that blew up bigger than anybody could ever have imagined.

Part One

Life is a beautiful struggle

—*Talib Kweli*

CHAPTER ONE

BORN ON THE ONE

New York City.

The Bronx, in particular.

Throgs Neck, to be even more specific.

2730 Dewey Avenue, to be exact.

December 31, 1960.

A few minutes before midnight. At midnight I'd be three—a New Year's baby.

Born on the one.

Born right on the beat.

I heard the beat. Should have been asleep, but the beats from my folks' house party had me wide awake.

Felt those beats all over me. Coming through the walls. Riding up the legs of my bed. The rhythms, the grooves, the get-down party in the next room where the lights were low and the folks were dancing.

Let me in there.

Let me in the party.

I peeked 'round the corner. I recognized a funky old organ jam but man, I wanted James Brown. James Brown had that jam where he screamed, "No, no, no, no, no . . . ," and I wanted to scream, wanted to jump in the middle of the action.

Like magic, my jam dropped. James started doing his thing and I started to get all crazy inside. Like I didn't ever want the beats to end.

I already knew house parties were for grown-ups. My dad—whose street name was Bra—made sure all us kids were down with the rules. The man had lots of rules. But right then, the crazy feeling inside me made up its own rules.

So I crept out the bedroom that I shared with my baby sister, Lilly. The hallway was dark but I could see the lights in the living room. Red and orange and blue. Could smell it too—swirling sweet and heavy in the air.

The beats that make the party.

Could almost see those beats. Could almost paint 'em, they were so clear. At the end of the hall, to the left, in the living room was the party. Everyone was vibing on James Brown, feet stomping, voices humming.

Pumping up the beats, building 'em up, keeping 'em strong.

So deep and so strong I had to get in there.

Had to be a part of it.

Suddenly I *was* there. Living room in front of me with the lights down low and smoke hanging from the ceiling. Family and friends, grinding and freaking, moving and grooving.

Every one of 'em in step with the beat.

When I saw what that smooth and solid beat could do, I was sold.

That's the memory.

The beat.

The beat that would become the heartbeat of my life.

FLASH'S UNIVERSAL DJ RULE NUMBER ONE

FLASH'S UNIVERSAL DJ RULE NUMBER ONE:
Don't stop the beat.

I was six and couldn't get enough of that beat.

The music would change whenever Dad went to the record store. Coming home with the new Sam and Dave, Stan Kenton, and Ella Fitzgerald. Throwing 'em on the phonograph and calling up the party people. Late at night, the beat was always there in the living room. Which meant I was too.

"Butsy crawlin' out the crib."

"Hey look, Butsy dancin' in his jammies."

"Ain't he cute?"

Butsy. That was my nickname. Or Nonny. Doin' that crazy little bug-out dance that kids do. That was me. Had to dance. Had to let it out. So I'd crawl up out the crib to get to the party people.

My older sisters Violet and Carmetta were cool, but they weren't into the scene. The girls got tired of late nights, loud noises, and cops coming around on complaints.

Police made you turn the music down. Turn it down or turn it off. Either way, it meant the party was over. Just that fast, everything stopped. But man, you can't stop the beat.

The source of the beat fascinated me like nothing else.

The record player!

The spin!

The thing that goes round and round! That thing was the secret to the beats!

Party or not, I would drag a chair over to the record player, climb up, and stare at it for hours.

How did this thing work?

Someone would hit the reject button. The arm would go up and the music would stop. The next record would drop and the beats would start all over again.

Magic!

Don't remember the first time I touched a record player, but I remember the first time I got caught. Wasn't a party night, just a Tuesday evening.

One of the Saddler rules was no children in the living room unless Mom and Dad were present. But the stereo was in that room. So I was too.

I'd defy the rules and sit there for hours listening to my father's records.

Bird.

Coltrane.

Monk, Mingus, and Miles.

Basie and Ellington.

Chuck Berry and Little Richard.

Don't know which sent me higher—the music or the mystery of how it played. I could hear the beats and feel the vibrations, but where did they come from? How did those funky sounds come out of the grooves on the disc? Through the needle? Down into the cabinet? How'd those paper cones behind the cloth speakers go *thump*? How did all those different sounds come out of there?

So I just sat for hours. Lost in the music, staring at the machine. Staring at the little red ON switch like it was a piece of candy, all lit up. Whatever made it glow was glowing inside me.

Wanted to control it. Manipulate it. Make it do what I said.

If I only knew how it worked!

Which was when my arm got pulled back. Hard. So hard it almost came out of my shoulder.

I forgot. It was already six o'clock. I'd lost track of time. My father was home. He yanked me right out of the chair with one hand and hit me across my face with the other. Before my feet even touched the ground.

"What I tell you about coming in here?"

WHAP!

"What I tell you about messin' with my stuff?"

WHAP!

When Dad saw me in the living room, it was enough for him to put a whuppin' on my butt and put my hand to the radiator.

"That'll teach you about messin' with my stuff!"

What really set him off was me messin' with his records. It wasn't the first time I'd been in trouble, but this was different. This really twisted his cap. This was personal, and the beating was bad. Mommy got in the middle of it—she always did—and shielded me from the blows. But there was only so much she could stop.

I avoided the hospital, but not by much.

It was the first of many beatings. Yet for all my pain, I was only thinking two things: one, this phonograph equipment must be some special stuff for him to kick my ass like that; two, don't ever stop the beat. So long as the music's playing, I'm safe.

Then came the beating of beatings.

DAD

I was almost seven. It was another Tuesday afternoon. It was cold out and the steam in the radiator was making the pipes rattle and hum. My hand was still sore from the last time Dad had put it there, but my fingers were tapping out a rhythm with the pipes that had me fiending for beats.

Violet was out with her boyfriend. Carmetta and my oldest sister, Regina, who we called Penny, were in their rooms. Mom had taken Lilly to the doctor, and Dad was at work.

Home alone. Just me and the music.

Mom and my sisters knew I was messin' with his stuff and told me not to, but I couldn't be stopped. One time, Penny asked me why I kept on messing with those records, bad as Dad hurt me.

Couldn't say. It was something I just had to do.

So I kept on doing it. I was big enough to reach the knob on the hall closet door, but needed a chair for the high shelves. That's where Dad kept all the good stuff. I knew there were jams at the top. I'd heard Dad and my big sister Violet say there was a new James Brown hit, and I had to hear it.

But the top shelf was way up high. Even standing on my dad's dining room chair—the one with the arms on it—I had to get on my tippy-toes and then, *sometimes*, I could reach the records I wanted to play.

Still, I could see the spine of the album cover, half an inch from my fingers. Close enough, I could feel its groove like electricity. So I jumped, got a hold, and pulled.

Got it!

But the record next to it fell to the floor and cracked into a hundred pieces. I looked down and saw it was Billy Eckstine's *Jelly Jelly*. JB might have survived the fall but *Jelly Jelly* was an old shellac 78. No way.

That's when I heard a key in the door. And one of the arms on the chair snapping. And me falling.

It was Dad.

Dad was a boxer, just like his brother Sandy. Sandy was especially bad; fact is, he was the featherweight champ of the world in 1950, retired with a hundred and three knockouts and later voted one of *The Ring* magazine's fifty greatest punchers of all time. Fighting spirit ran in the family.

Dad was also a track man. He'd come home early from his gig with the Penn Central Railroad and he was shouting, *"Who's in my closet? Who's messing with my records?"* Soon as he saw me and his shattered record, he grabbed my neck, lifted me off the floor, dragged me out of the closet, then let me have it for real.

Dad knocked me clean across the hall with a slap from his hand, his skin rough as sandpaper. Next thing I remember was waking up. Mommy was screaming and Lilly was crying. There was blood all over the front of my shirt and a ringing in my ears.

When Mommy had come home and tried to stop Dad, he went at her with an iron skillet. Beat on her until he finally busted her head open. Both of 'em screaming so loud, a neighbor finally called the cops. The cops knew where we lived, and by then my father knew the drill—he skipped out before they came, leaving them to deal with Mommy. Disappearing back out into the street life; back into the bars and boxing gyms he loved more than home.

Days later he'd show up, arms full of groceries, acting like everything was okay. But the violence would start up all over again just as soon as Mommy started yelling and screaming how he was layed up with other women. Lots of 'em.

She knew 'cause sometimes they came to our door, pregnant and saying Dad was the daddy. Saying he was with her now. Asking when he'd be home. Nobody ever saw a four-foot-eleven woman raise such hell as Mommy did when that happened.

She'd curse him so bad it was only a matter of time before he started beating on her again. But no matter how hard he beat her, she never pressed charges. No matter how many times other women came around, she never left him.

Maybe she loved him too much.

Or maybe she was too scared.

Might have been the beating or it might have been the cheating, but my mother was not a well woman for most of my life. The more my father beat me, the more he beat her. And the more he beat her, the more unstable she got. The more unstable she got, the less he came around home. And the less he came around home, the less of a home we had.

SPIN

That was the spin in the Saddler house when I was little.

Like the wheels of my bike, a metallic green Huffy with a white banana seat. Mom bought it for me using S&H Green Stamps. Saved 'em up for over a year. It was the baddest bike in the neighborhood, but I never even learned to ride it.

Instead, I turned the bike upside down and spun the wheels with my hands. For hours and hours at a time. Penny and Mommy would always tell me to get on the seat and go somewhere, but I never did. I was happy to watch the wheels go 'round.

Watching 'em spin. Ones and twos.

Counting the spokes. Putting a playing card in each wheel and listening to 'em go *tat-tat-tat-tat-tat-tat-tat-tat-tat-tat.*

Tattin' out a beat. 90 ... 100 ... 110 times a minute. Speedin' 'em up. Slowin' 'em down. Gettin' 'em in time with each other.

It was just as hypnotic as the spinning record player and the music, but these wheels of steel were all mine. I could control 'em.

Wished I had that same control over the record player. Wished I had the same control over the beats.

Wished I had the same control over my sisters.

To begin with, I was the only boy in a house full of girls. Four of 'em.

Four against one is never a fair fight and my sisters knew it. Whatever they wanted, they could get me to do it. If you have four girls bugging you to take out the trash or go to the store, you're in trouble. Sooner or later you do what they say, even if it's just to get 'em quiet.

I might not have been tough, but I was smart. They might break me down to run to the store, but I always got some free candy and pop outta the deal.

When they ganged up on me, I learned quick what happens when bossy girls don't get what they want—and I ran away fast. Dress-up party? I was gone in a flash. You wanna do *what* with my hair? I was gone even quicker.

I would just spin out. Might not have made me a good little brother, but it sure was fun to get mixed up in their business. Any records they had were mine, far as I was concerned. They were deep into Aretha and the Supremes and the Ronettes. I couldn't get enough of Ronnie Spector's voice. My favorite thing to do was to put on "Be My Baby," then run around the house while my sisters chased me.

Violet was the worst. Like Dad, she was always saying I didn't have respect for anyone's stuff. She yelled loud, hit hard, and could have a mean temper if she wanted.

Violet was just like our Dad.

It made sense. Violet was the oldest and she was his favorite. They were close; whatever violence my father brought in the house, she never put it on him, 'cause he never put it on her. Violet and Dad had a special bond.

Like Dad, Violet had a taste for the nightlife. Me and Lilly and Penny would watch her get ready and we knew there was something special out there. She'd bring home fox furs and chinchillas and have Mommy sew 'em on to her leather boots and coat collars. Nobody had anything on my big sister Violet when it came to style.

Carmetta hung back and did her own thing, and didn't mess with me much. If I let her be, she'd do the same, but if I gave her any mess at all, she'd lose it. And unlike Penny and Violet, Carmetta gave better chase. If she caught up, she'd let me know she didn't stand for being played a fool. At the same time, Carmetta could be real cool. When we were the only ones home, she'd talk to me about what music was hip and what music was square. I'd tell her I liked Duke Ellington and Count Basie—Dad liked those guys—and she'd set me straight. She'd tell me why I should be listening to Tito Puente and the Temptations instead.

Then there was Penny. She was only two years older than me, but she was born tough, so she might as well have been a second mother to me and Lilly.

Penny was a lot like Mommy. Penny was born to be a mom. She watched over me no matter how much trouble I caused. She yelled and screamed sometimes, but if she gave me a hard time, it was for my own good. If Penny got mad, it was because I was messin' up, not because I was messin' her over.

Penny also hated Dad for what he did to me and Mommy. Maybe she couldn't stop him from beating on us, but she could stop anyone else from beating on me, and she did. What she didn't start with her fists, Penny could finish with her mouth, or the other way around—Penny always had a tongue like fire and wasn't afraid to use it, even if it got her in trouble. Throughout it all, my big sis was always there for me.

I always loved her for that.

As for me and my baby sister, Lilly, we were tight—real tight—but whatever my big sisters put on me by way of torture, I turned around and put right back on her. When a bully from Lilly's school came around saying she wanted to fight, my little sister ran back into the bedroom and hid. I threw her down on the bed, yanked on her shoes, then got in her face. I had already taught her what Dad had taught me—your power comes from your shoulder, not your arm—and now it was time to use it.

I told her straight up: "If you don't go out there and defend yourself, I'm gonna whup you myself."

Lilly went out and clobbered that girl.

It might have been tough love, but it wasn't nothing Penny hadn't put on me. Besides, in Lilly's eyes, I could do no wrong. And for all the messing her around I did, I loved her like crazy too. Lilly just wanted somebody to belong to, same as me. And though Mommy and Dad didn't always fit the bill, at least we had Penny. At least we had each other.

One day, Dad just up and left. I was almost eight. The man got in his car and never came back. He didn't say good-bye, I love you, or I'm still your

Daddy. He just left, and took most of his records with him. Said he'd return for the rest later, but he never did.

Maybe his leaving really was about me messing with his records—the man did love his music. Maybe my father was jealous—I was Mommy's favorite and he always said she spoiled me. Maybe he was mad—I was always crawling in bed when he was trying get some play. Maybe he wanted out—having a family, especially a son, never seemed to make him all that happy.

Or maybe he was just mean.

At least now I could mess with the records he left without getting caught. But Dad spun out with the turntable before anything else.

With no Dad and no record player, the house was quiet—rough times.

When neighbors downstairs would play music, I'd put my ear to the floor to hear the sounds vibing up through the hardwood. Diana Ross and the sweet siren sounds of the Supremes sighing that "Baby Love" to me. Ray Charles hollering out, "I Can't Stop Lovin' You."

Wonder if Dad had stopped loving me.

Even with the beams and boards blocking the way, I'd lie there for hours, trying to pick out the songs and sounds I missed so much, tapping out rhythms with my fingers in time.

Anything to keep the beat.

I had to find my own way to play the records.

A blackout helped me to do it. The Northeast Blackout of 1965. I was eight. It was the biggest blackout ever—no power all the way up to Canada. By the time the sun went down, Mommy wasn't home—she got stuck on the subway—so Penny told me and Lilly to stay in the house while she went out to look for something for us to eat.

Everything was dark.

Nothing worked.

There was nothing to do but sit.

I was real messed up about it—not only did we have no record player, now we didn't have no power either! I got so bored, I put a record on the wheel of my bike and started spinning.

If we didn't have a turntable or any power, at least I could pretend. But then I got to thinking about how the whole thing worked as I spun the record around on the bike wheel. I knew the records went around and around. And I knew the little needle had something to do with making the sound come out.

So I went to Mom's sewing kit and got the smallest safety pin she had. As the record was spinning, I put the pin in the groove and held it there. It didn't sound like it was supposed to, but *something* was making the needle vibe.

Science and music make magic.

Penny came in the door right around then and looked at what I was doing.

"How'd you think to do that?" she asked.

I couldn't give her an answer. "Just did it," was all I could tell her.

Then one beautiful day a few weeks before Christmas, Mommy came home with a record player along with some Nat Cole records. Hallelu- jah! That made everyone's holiday. I remember listening to Nat sing "The Christmas Song" over and over again. No violence. No drama. No yelling. Just peace and quiet. Sitting there in the living room, Mommy would hug and kiss me and call me her baby boy while the girls danced around the room. And for a week or two before Christmas of 1965, everything was cool.

But that didn't last. Mom's moods were too unstable, too hard to pre- dict. One minute everything would be okay, and then she'd be screaming at the top of her lungs. No words. No stopping to catch her breath. Just straight-up blind rage.

And it wasn't just screaming either. Mom got violent. Never to me or my sisters, but to anyone else who caught her on the wrong minute. A woman at the grocery store would ask my mother to hold her place in line and my mother would go upside her head with a can of corn. The downstairs neighbors would tell her not to move the furniture at three in the morning and Mom would go banging on their front door with her fist. And on the few occasions Dad would come around with some food, Mom would get so angry, she'd throw his stuff down the incinerator. Imagine that: a grown woman throwing perfectly good food away. Didn't make any sense to me, but she claimed anything he put his hands on was just as evil as he was.

No evil food in the house.

No evil furniture in the house.

No evil coats and shoes in the house.

So instead, we went hungry, cold, and barefoot. Times got harder. Mommy was resourceful—she could make dumplings out of flour and pork fat and stretch government cheese, peanut butter, and Spam further than anybody—but when you got five kids and two jobs and not enough welfare to cover your nut, things get hard. And when things got hard, Mommy would start up all over again.

Someone would always call the cops. Except without my father around, Mom would fight the police instead. She'd fight anyone who told her what to do.

Pretty soon, the wheels would be spinning again. Only this time, they'd be bringing the ambulances and the orderlies with the straitjackets. The orderlies would pump her full of tranquilizers, take her to Pilgrim State Hospital. They said it was a place for people like her.

But when would she be back? No one knew.

Sometimes Mom's sister—my aunt Mary—would take us in. Mary and her kids—my cousins Kourduanii, Kyel, and Armel—were black Jews and went to synagogue on 125th Street. When Mom was in the hospital, Lilly, Penny, and I would go with them on Saturdays.

At the synagogue, we learned about the Torah and the Talmud. We learned about Moses and Abraham and the Old Testament. Aunt Mary taught us all about the Jewish high holidays.

I can't say I turned into a believer, but I didn't mind going. Having a preacher who wasn't a preacher but a black rabbi—Rabbi Mathews was his name—was an interesting experience. It was different, and I've never minded being different.

One Rosh Hashanah, Lilly and I followed the whole congregation down to Riverside Park to purge an apple in the Hudson River for a clean new year. As the ceremony started, a boatload of kids mooned us and shouted some stuff about us being black and Jewish. Aunt Mary tried to tell us that we were all God's children and that we were all brothers and sisters, Jews or otherwise, but if that was true, how come she was Jewish and Mom wasn't?

As for Mom, I don't know much about mental illness or why my mother had it, but she kept going in and out of that hospital, kept getting shock treatments, and kept coming home zombified. She'd be fine for a few days or weeks, but then she'd make a scene and the whole thing would start over again. As time went on, she was in the hospital more than out.

One time she came home and began to paint everything gray: the walls, the windows, the couches, the tables and chairs; even our coats got slathered with gray house paint. Everything in the kitchen was that one color gray. It was scary 'cause it didn't make any sense. All we knew was, something was really wrong with Mommy. Penny would try to tell us it was no big deal, but me and Lilly knew better—Mommy was sick. I had an idea it was because gray was probably the color of everything at Pilgrim State . . . but I didn't say nothing.

Eventually, somebody told social services there were no suitable adults around, and a lady from the Department of Child Welfare came to our apartment in a white van. Came one morning while me and Lilly and Jackie—one of the older kids in the building—were out front playing Vietnam. Jackie had just been drafted, and even though he had on a uniform he still let me and Lilly be the Americans.

A year had gone by since Dad left and I was almost nine.

There hadn't been hardly any food in the cupboard. Penny had been rubbing grease on our lips; when we were starving, me and Lilly's lips got all white and cracked, and the grease hid it. But the grease didn't hide the fact there were no adults around.

Since Violet and Carmetta were in their late teens, the lady said they were old enough to take care of themselves, "but these three here gotta go."

My older sisters fought to keep Penny and me and Lilly.

But rules was rules.

ANOTHER PLANET

They put me and Lilly and Penny in that white van and took us away to foster homes in the Bronx.

It was especially hard for Lilly—Penny and I were old enough to understand a little better. But to Lilly, the baby, our place on Dewey Avenue was the whole world. She cried like hell in the back of that van and I hated the sound of it. Hated that I couldn't stop it.

Sometimes the foster families were okay. Sometimes they weren't. Either way, I'd leave out almost as quick as I got there, running back to the people and the places I knew in Throgs Neck.

When me and Lilly were in the same foster home, we'd run away together. So they started splitting us up and spinning us out farther away from home, either way down to Lower Manhattan or way up to the top of Harlem.

But we'd always find each other.

We knew our way around. Lilly might have been sheltered, but she was no fool when she wanted something bad enough. And Penny—like always—could take care of herself.

We'd meet in a familiar place—a park or a store—then jump a train back to the Bronx. It was like a game:

1. Escape from behind enemy lines.
2. Hook up.
3. Head home.

It went on like that for almost a year. Those white vans showed up so many times and we escaped so many places that I don't remember hardly any of the faces or the names of those foster families.

There were a couple times when somebody had a turntable and some records. I'd stick around long enough to go through everything they had and discover some good jams—from the Contours' "First I Look at the Purse" to the Gypsies' "Jerk It." But then me and Lilly would be gone.

Finally, the caseworker took desperate measures.

"We're takin' y'all out to the country."
Say what?
Caseworker said we were gonna live with some white family up in Newburgh, way beyond the North Bronx. I had heard about the country, but seeing it for real was a trip.
They got jams out here?
That's what I was thinking as the caseworker drove us into the sticks, this time in her own car instead of the van. When she let me pick the music on the ride, the Four Tops made promises with "I'll Be There," even if nobody was here for me and Lilly and Penny. Percy Sledge moaned about what it's like "When a Man Loves a Woman," but I knew he wasn't talking about Mommy and Bra.

The further we got outta the city, the more my music turned to static. By the time we got where we were going, the radio didn't do nothing but buzz. So did my head.

We might as well have been on another planet. Nobody was black and the people there looked so different, there was no way they could be listening to jams like we had in the city.

I was right.

Instead of music, me and Lilly and Penny got a cow.

Child Welfare figured to put us so far from home, we couldn't run away. We ended up with a white foster family on a dairy farm. That was bad enough, but when the dad told me I had to wash, feed, and milk an animal, I threw a fit. Screamed at him louder than I ever had in my life; even Penny was scared.

I figured they could take me away from home, make me live on a farm, but I ain't milking no cow.

We wound up at another place, this one called the Greer School at Hope Farm, not far from Poughkeepsie. I was scared it was gonna be the worst place yet, but I was all wrong. Fact is, me and Lilly loved it, even if Penny didn't.

First off, it was on this huge piece of land covered with hills and valleys and pastures and creeks and streams. And right there in the middle of all that was the Greer School for Boys and Girls.

We lived in these dorms they called cottages, boys on one side of the farm and girls on the other, but otherwise it was blacks and whites all mixed together. The Greer School was hundreds of kids from all kinds of backgrounds. Might not have all been kids who got whupped by their dads. Might not have all been kids who got abandoned or kids whose moms were sick. But nobody at the Greer School ever made me and my sisters feel anything other than right at home.

The people who ran it were nice too. They listened to you. Tried to get to know you. There were houseparents to watch over us and local families to take us in at the holidays when nobody else did. Nobody was too tough, and they didn't put one on your ass if you made a mistake.

Penny missed the city too much. She had developed a taste for partying. With no fences and no walls, she ran away within the first few months we were there and ended up staying with our grandma back in the Bronx. When I found out, I thought about doing the same, but the truth was I didn't want to go. The Greer School had become cool.

I even got my first shot at controlling the music at a party up there. Every year, we organized a Halloween dance. One of the houseparents—Missus Dot—had a portable turntable and a decent collection of 45s. Thanks to Penny, Missus Dot knew I had a big thing for record players and tunes. When she asked me if I wanted to be in charge of the music, I went for it.

One of the 45s was by James Brown's man Bobby Byrd. It was called "I Know You Got Soul," and when I threw it on, something magical happened—people stopped milling about the food table, got up from their chairs, moved out of the corners of the gym, and started to groove. It was a big moment, and a big reminder of the house parties back on Dewey Ave.

Never missed a chance to be the disc jockey at a Greer School dance after that.

Up at Greer, there was also camping in the summers and sledding in the winters, shop classes, learning to bake our own bread, Friday night movies in the barn, chasing bats out of the icehouse, which I loved, 'cause I was always the fastest runner at school.

Magic times.

Greer was more than just a school. For almost five years between 1966 and 1971, Greer was home.

But even if it was a cool home, it wasn't my home. I realized that one day when I was on a grocery run.

The country was still the country. Kids were into music, but it was stuff like the Byrds and the Beatles and Jimi Hendrix. That stuff was cool, especially Hendrix, but about as funky as the radio got was the Isley Brothers and the Temptations and Aretha and I already knew that stuff backward and forward.

I wanted new jams. I wanted stuff I'd never heard before.

Then one day I went into town with a couple of the older kids to get food at the A&P.

I was already excited about the trip. But once we got to town, something happened. Something that gave me what I was looking for.

Stopped at the light next to us, a car full of kids was blasting the funkiest jam I'd ever heard. Had a psychedelic soul groove that grabbed my ear and almost tore it off.

"What is that?" I asked the dude driving the car.

"Sly and the Family Stone. 'Dance to the Music.' "

"New?"

"Nope. Almost three years old. Where you been, man?"

Where *had* I been? Out there in the country, there wasn't any yelling and fighting. Out there at the Greer School, I got to know a lot of good people. I got to learn a valuable lesson: that people are people—black, white, or otherwise. Nobody judged me by the color of my skin, a lesson I've carried with me since.

But up at Greer, I was missing the beat.

As soon as I realized that, I knew I had to get back to the Bronx.

SPIN BACK

My instinct was right on time because my mother got out of Pilgrim State a couple weeks before me and Lilly arrived home. She seemed fine. Whether it was a new medication, something in the air, or just the grace of God, they let her go. Even more of a miracle was that she got us back.

Yet nothing was the same.

For starters, we didn't stay in Throgs Neck anymore. Mom and the girls had already moved to Fox Street and 163rd, near Fort Apache.

The South Bronx.

This was the early seventies, when they called the South Bronx hell on earth. Even the cops were afraid to go there.

Nearly every kid my age was running with a gang. Biggest ones in my area were the Savage Skulls, the Black Pearls, and the Black Spades. These three ran everything. If people had a problem in the neighborhood, they went to the gangs before they went to the cops. Other gangs—the Seven Immortals, the Savage Nomads, the Roman Kings, Ghetto Brothers, and the Persuaders—were nothing to fuck with either.

They were wall-to-wall hardrocks, lookin' like black and Puerto Rican Hell's Angels. Flyin' colors and cut sleeves and letting you know if you didn't have permission to go around that way, you were gonna get stomped. I saw how territory and respect were serious business—violate either and you'd get a serious beatdown and have your sneakers thrown up over a lightpole.

Those were the days of turf wars, junkie massacres, and all kinds of crazy drama. 163rd and Fox was ground zero.

Just like Greer had been a whole other world for me, now the Bronx was a whole other world all over again. "How come you sound like you're white?" the other kids would ask. I'd been away during the time my peers were learning how to walk, talk, and act on the streets. The Greer School had kept me innocent.

So while I joined a gang for a short while, the shit just didn't interest me. And at the time, neither did drugs. I had a good instinct for avoiding that stuff—I knew I had no business with either. Might have been God looking out, but being up at Greer showed me there was more to life than knocking heads.

Still, where did I fit in?

I didn't even know where I fit in my own family. Bra wasn't around. Aunt Mary and her kids told us we were still welcome, but Mom got mad. Mom came home from Pilgrim State clearer in her mind, but now she was crazy for Jesus. She was pressing us hard to accept Jesus as our personal lord and saviour, yelling how if we didn't, we were going to hell. But what she was saying didn't jibe with what I'd learned at the synagogue over in Harlem.

On the other hand, Violet and Carmetta had become Jehovah's Witnesses. They found a home at the Kingdom Hall and were hardcore in their beliefs. Sometimes they took Lilly and me along. I liked some things I heard, but I can't say I jumped in feet first. Kingdom Hall was cool, but I still didn't feel it was moving my spirit.

Who—or what—was I supposed to believe?

My head was into music and electronics. Both lit me up, but both things were as far apart as anything in my world.

With the music, it was simple and pure. I rode the beat and enjoyed the high. That's how music is—either you feel it or you don't. I learned that from my dad's house parties, and I knew what the right song could do to a crowd.

Except I wasn't interested in the actual making of music. Beats and grooves were cool, but I wasn't one of those guys who picked up an instrument and instantly knew what to do.

But electronics were different. Electronics drew me in. It was still an emotional thing, but more in my head than in my gut.

Take record players, for example. Record players still rocked me. I knew the needle sat in the groove as the vinyl went around. I knew the grooves made the needle vibrate and the needle sent the vibes out to the speakers. I knew all those colored boxes and bulbs and tubes and windings inside the stereo had something to do with it, but I didn't know what. I knew what electricity was, but I didn't know how it worked.

If I could figure out how to jump a subway train, though; if I could figure out how to build a teepee and bake biscuits for two hundred kids, I could learn audio technology.

But where?

I'd start at home.

I started with things like hair dryers and straightening irons. Then I'd go inside the washing machine and the ceiling fan to see how they spun. Then I'd take apart somebody's stereo. Plus the speakers. Had to break open the TV. Two or three times. And when there was nothing left to dismantle, I messed with the light fixtures and wall switches.

If it plugged in the wall, ran on batteries, or had moving parts, I started messing with it. Takin' it apart. Puttin' it back together. Pissin' off Penny and Carmetta like nobody's business.

"Who the hell broke my radio?"

"BUTSEEEEEEEEEEY!"

"Butsy did it! I saw him jackin' it up just the other day! Saw him taking it apart like Frankenstein!"

"Butsy, you little punk! Quit messin' with my stuff!"

"You leave your brother alone," Mom would say. "He can fix it!"

Mom was a trouper. Even if I couldn't fix any of that shit, she always believed in me.

Mom was an ingenious seamstress, so she understood craft, technique, and creativity. She understood me. She knew if I was gonna make sense of this stuff, I needed some school.

And school changed everything.

Samuel Gompers Vocational Technical was a high school up in Fort Apache. Thank God for Samuel Gompers. Other kids there might have been passing the time, but I loved it. The teachers had answers. They knew the functions of all the colorful boxes, bubbles, and blobs inside the phonograph. They showed me how a resistor controls the voltage. How a capacitor changes AC to DC. They broke it all down, and I was deep into it—I got As without even trying.

What interested me most was stereo stuff. Just when I thought I had all the answers, a dozen new questions would come up. What does a tuner do? Why do you need a preamp? How do all the components work together?

How do they make the beats?

Now when I tore into something, I had an understanding of how it worked. Now I could tell you why vacuum tubes produced better sound quality than transistors, but why transistors were the new thing.

When I wasn't up in class, I kept schooling myself at home. Toasters and waffle makers were old news ever since I'd found a broken stereo in the street. The goal was to see if I could bring it back to life. I tried to jerry-rig it, but all I got was a weak buzz that sounded like a nest of angry bees. It pissed off everybody, except Mom.

It was a start, but if I wanted real music, I needed more than a busted-up radio. By now, my sisters wouldn't let me within ten feet of their record player. I swore if I couldn't beg, borrow, or steal a sound system from somewhere, I'd make my own.

Besides, building something from scratch was on a whole other level. And that's where I wanted to be.

So I was ready for my first assignment in the tenth grade: building a tube amplifier from scratch. At the heart of the project were the 12AX7 tubes, the push-pull circuit, and the step-down transformers. I was fascinated with how they worked.

But I wanted to do even more; I wanted to build an entire sound system. Only one problem:

Where would I get the parts?

No job and no money meant having nothing to work with, and stereo components didn't grow on trees. What I needed was out there, though; I just had to go hunt it down.

Back in the early seventies, garbage collectors left all kinds of stuff in the vacant lots around the Bronx instead of taking it to the scrap yard or city dump. People would make noise about how it was illegal and unsafe for the kids, but to me it was like they turned my neighborhood into a gold mine. All I had to do was dig.

On my way home from school, a pair of wire cutters in one hand and a screwdriver in the other, I'd be on the lookout for any piece of usable circuitry I could find. I'd root through junk piles and garbage heaps, but old cars were always the best.

Fortunately there were burned-out jalopies all over the place. I quickly discovered that 6x9s and 5½-inch speakers were easy to come by—just look behind the backseat and in the doors. Radios would usually be gone if the car was stripped, but it was wild how many speakers would be left over. I found so many I could pick and choose—you only take ones with the cones intact. I'd even follow the wires back to the dash and get ten feet of cable. If I did find a car radio, it was usually good for a few resistors and capacitors, which would prevent a speaker from surging and blowing out if I wired it up wrong.

The best score was my first real turntable, and finding it was like winning the lottery. Here's how it went down:

I was comin' home from school, doin' my thing, but none of my spots were turning up anything good. After a couple hours of that, I was ready to go home.

That was when I saw Duck from around the way going corner to corner, trying to pawn what he was holding. It was getting dark and I couldn't see what he had in his hands, but something in my gut said to follow.

Duck was getting as much love from the street as I was, which meant none. Whatever he had was square and flat with cord wrapped around the middle, and the corner boys wouldn't have shit to do with it. He'd offer it up, get a few looks, but they'd all brush him off. At one point, somebody took it, plugged it in, and gave it a second, but walked away and told him to jet.

My man eventually gave up and chucked it out. I made my move. There at my feet was a used but decent belt-driven Thorens turntable. One of the newer styles with an aluminum platter. Couldn't have been more than a year old. Whatever was wrong with it, I could fix.

My heart started racing.

Man, I'm in business.

YELLOW NUTS ON A COLD NIGHT

I'm sitting in class a week later, working on my amp. Figuring out how the push-pull circuits are supposed to drive the current. Compared to professional stuff, my little amp's nothing nice, but at least I'm doing it. And once it's done, I'll be one step closer to having my own sound system.

I'm the only one in class. Nobody else cares enough to show up, but I can't stay away. Sometimes I don't even hear the bell, I just work through recess, lunch, and all my other classes.

Have to finish the amp. Don't care how long it takes.

Only thing that keeps me on time is the 5 train outside. Every time it rumbles down the track, I look up.

I'm pissed at first 'cause it takes me out of my work groove—the damn train won't be quiet. Keeps shouting at me to pay attention. A couple hours of looking up every few minutes and it hits me: The line's totally bombed. And when I say bombed, I mean completely spray-painted.

Every train.

Every car.

Every square inch.

Twelve by sixty feet. Eight times over. Covered top-to-bottom by those graffiti dudes.

Dudes like LEE.

PHASE 2.

TAKI 183.

SUPER KOOL 223.

STAY HIGH 149.

Giant machines covered in art. Covered in style.

Styles so wild, you can hardly keep up. Letters and numbers so worked up, it takes a minute to figure out where one stops and the next one begins. Like some kind of alien alphabet.

The colors explode, drip, drift, smash, clash, bleed, and crackle with energy fields. They create images of cartoon action heroes at crazy angles. They invent new shapes and designs like nobody's ever seen before.

Sometimes you gotta step back and look at it sideways, 'cause you only see the tip of the iceberg. Just a little piece of a letter, a face, an object; making up a word, making up a sentence, making up a scene. One train's carrying a message that says:

"IF ART IS A CRIME, MAY GOD FORGIVE ME."

I can dig it.

I can also dig what it takes to get those murals done. Means sneaking into the Ghost Yard—the 207th Street lay-up—in the middle of the night. Lugging a forty-pound duffel bag forty blocks north and scaling barbed-wire fences. Means going to jail if you get caught. Means fighting off other crews for trains.

Graffiti writing is a battle for supremacy. All weaklings get dissed.

Graffiti writing is a war.

And in a war, there's strategies, tactics, weapons, and rules. Tags are everywhere. On walls and park benches. On windows and on doors.

In the war, tags are like the foot soldiers—you put as many as you can out on the battlefield. Tagging is how you get your name out. Tagging's everywhere.

When you bomb a wall or a train, it's like your castle, your spray-paint kingdom. And just like your home, you protect that shit 'cause it takes so long to build.

Then there's throw-ups. Big bubbled letters, fancier than a tag, but not as intricate as a full-on piece. Dusty ones, solid ones, ones with shadows, ones without, skinny caps, fat caps, flares—there's all kinds. Throw-ups are like the artillery—tanks and fighter jets. Throw-ups are how you beef.

Maybe you go out one night and crush a train. Maybe you crush a whole lay-up yard to prove how you're the man. The very next night, some other dude rolls up with his paint, and in five minutes he's going over you, destroying your castle. Spitting on your face. Throwin' up and filling in what it took you all night to create. Making it like you were never even there.

Now you got an enemy. He's on you and you're on him—going over each other for life.

An art war.

Insane!

But the respect those cats got—oh man! Because of the trains, they were known and respected all over the city. They *had* to be, dangerous like it was.

You couldn't help but bow down for what it took to be out there.

Bow down to a cat who was doing something you could feel.

Bow down to a cat with something to say.

So when STAY HIGH snuck into a hangar at JFK and hit up a TWA jet, it made the national evening news. That's when I decided I had to get on the case. My electronics could wait a minute.

I went behind my building where nobody would see me and I started to write graffiti.

FLASH 163

Flash was the nickname given to me by my friend Gordon Upshaw, who also lived on Fox Street. Because we both liked Flash Gordon cartoons—and he was already Gordon—and because I could run real fast. One-sixty-three was the Ave where I lived—that's how the other writers did it. That's how you let everyone know where you were from.

In my head, FLASH 163 looked like a bad-ass tag. When I saw it on the wall it looked like shit. I couldn't get the letters to make the same shapes comin' out of the spray can. I couldn't get the spacing down so that it looked right.

This wasn't like my music and my electronics. Wasn't feeling the beat in graffiti.

I wasn't about to give up, though. I got my hands on a can of black Krylon and practiced until my name looked halfway cool. Couple days later I tagged FLASH 163 on every wall and curb for a couple blocks around my house, thinking that now *I* was the man.

But I wasn't fooling anyone—myself included.

Almost immediately I started getting crossed out, gone over, and labeled either HOT 110, meaning you're a whack nobody, or DGA—Don't Get Around.

I didn't get around.

Maybe I had to step it up. Start my own beef. But then my friend OG told me a story about a dude he knew:

"You know my man who's writin' CREAM? Just the other day, he went up to the Ghost Yard, saying how he was gonna crush a train. Another crew steps to him, sayin' how that particular train on that particular line was personal property. If he could be a gentleman about it, they said they'd let him go with just a warning."

"For real?" I said. "What he do?"

"Put up a fight. But they flipped him, pulled down his pants, and spray-painted his balls yellow. Then they made him go outta there like that too—no drawers and yellow nuts on a cold night."

Oh shit!

It was easy to think how OG's man was a chump. No way would I get played like that. But no way was I gonna take my chances going up to that yard either, not after what happened to CREAM.

I was writing my name like a hero, but getting crossed out like a sucker.

Truth was, I wasn't painting any top-to-bottoms, my writing style was foul, and my name wasn't getting around. I wasn't beefin' with other writers or taking any other risks to get a rep.

Maybe God didn't want me to be a graffiti artist. But that didn't mean I didn't still feel those dudes. They spoke to me louder than ever, just not in my language.

I had to find a language of my own.

So I went home, grabbed my soldering iron, and got back to work.

PORK BARRELS & BEST FRIENDS

Mom loved me, but she hated the pork barrels. She hated pork, period. If it had anything to do with a pig, Mom would flip out.

One day, I brought home these big plastic containers used to ship bacon sides that I'd found in the dumpster behind the meat shop. Three days later, the whole house smelled like rotten meat; I had promised my mother I'd wash 'em out but never got around to it. Now she wouldn't let me keep my stuff at the house, and I wasn't allowed to bring home any more junk.

"Enough is enough!" she screamed.

"But those barrels are gonna be perfect speaker cabinets, Ma!" My plan was to mount all the best speakers I had down inside and stuff a couple pillows in the dead space to maximize the acoustics, then glue them in. "Please! I'll put bay leaves and orange peels down in there, just let me keep 'em!"

Mom refused and now I had nowhere to work.

That's when my best friends stepped in.

Thank God I didn't take to the gangs harder. Thank God I was into something different. Thank God for Truman and OJ and E-Z Mike.

I was only back from the Greer School a few weeks and I started notic-ing E-Z Mike wherever I went. If I went to the store for my mom, walked home from Gompers, or just bummed around for junk, there was E-Z Mike, bumming around on his own. Mike looked like a friendly enough guy, but you didn't go up and just talk to anybody in the South Bronx.

But one day, I said "hey" to him. Without blinking, Mike threw me a sly and easy smile, like somehow he knew we were gonna get along just fine. That smile said he was the most laid-back cat ever. Mike was like that, and if you got the smile, you were on his good side for life.

Mike introduced me to the other two guys I'd already seen around. I'd be on my way to school and I'd see OJ shooting dice. I couldn't walk down the hall in my apartment without bumping into Truman, who'd be trying to get some play from one of the girls in the building. I met Mon-key George through Truman. And it didn't take long for Flash, Truman, Monkey George, OJ, and E-Z Mike to buddy up.

One of the things that made us tight was music. Those guys were into the same jams I was. I remember OJ laying the Ohio Players' *Fire* LP on me and I thought I'd died and gone to heaven. Truman hit me with the Jacksons' *Lookin' Through the Windows*, and Mike saved the best for last with Stevie Wonder's *Innervisions*; the sounds Stevie spun out were strange and lovely and went straight from my ear to my heart.

Truman heard about what happened with my mom banning my junk and told his pop. Turned out Pops was the super of a brownstone over on Faille Street and the basement was empty. He said that so long as we didn't tell anybody, we could use it as a clubhouse.

That basement could have been a rusted tin shed with a leaky roof and it would have been Shangri-la to me, Truman, OJ, Monkey George, and E-Z Mike.

Turned out it wasn't half bad either—it was probably twenty-five by thirty feet, had its own entrance from the back lot, some sawhorse tables, and all the electrical outlets I needed.

Soon as I got all my stuff outta the house, I got to work rigging the joint for sound. I still had way more junked speakers than I had cabinets and boxes, so I twisted wire hangers around the speaker frames and hung 'em all over the ceiling; so much that it started to look like a mess of spiderwebs. But now I could fill the joint with the sweet soul sounds of Smokey Robinson and the Miracles.

Those slow jams helped Mike see the real potential on Faille Street.

"We can start throwing parties down here," he said. "We could put up Christmas lights for dancing but we still keep the rest of it real dark. That way, we can get the girls going in the little rooms. We get some old couches and a mattress and this spot could be raw."

"The girls" were the Dawson sisters. I was dating Paulette, Mike was dating the one called Cynthia, Truman had Debra, and OJ went out with Barbara. And since they traveled as a crew, so did we. The girls were the other reason we hung out all the time.

And Faille Street *was* raw when we finally finished decking it out. It'd be like going down into a whole other world, especially if the tunes were going. Isaac and Marvin. The O'Jays and Eddie Kendricks. The Chi-Lites and the Temptations. Gladys Knight and the Pips. There were Christmas lights strung up on the equipment table and around the main support columns in the middle of the room. The windows were blacked out. The whole thing was a subterranean lair, complete with couches and a ratty old mattress.

Matter of fact, I lost my virginity down there.

At sixteen, I was starting to shed my geekiness and notice girls. The girl was Paulette Dawson. Paulette was eighteen, older than me, and already curvy and thick in all the right ways. She was also smart—smarter than any other girl I knew—and could carry on a conversation about all kinds of stuff. Most of all, she was interested in me.

But Penny knew better. I might have just fallen back off the hay wagon after coming home from Greer, but Penny had been around the whole time and knew what girls were like, especially when they wanted something.

Mom was even less sure about Paulette. She knew even better than Penny what was coming. Paulette *was* older than me, and in my mother's book, that was a strike—strike one. She didn't see the two of us together as natural. Strike two was Paulette's aggressiveness. She would come around Fox Street looking for me when I wasn't looking for her. (I was usually out looking for my electronics, which always took the front seat to getting with the other sex.)

"Is Flash home, Mrs. Saddler?"

"No."

"Well, could you tell him I was here, please?"

"No." Paulette was always polite, but Mrs. Saddler wasn't having it, and whenever she got the chance, she'd tell me to my face: "Girl's too experienced for you."

Mom knew that experienced girls gave it up. Especially if there was a place to go get it on. And me and Paulette most definitely had a place to go, over on Faille Street.

But first and foremost, Joseph Saddler had a place to go. I had a place to experiment with my electronics to my heart's content and a place to groove on my jams, down in my dark and dusty soul den.

And then, just like that, my whole world did a backflip.

BREAK

It was 1975 and I was seventeen. The TV had pictures of Gerald Ford—the new president who pardoned President Nixon—talking about some upcoming two hundredth American birthday shit, but the paper was telling us that he'd dissed the city. "Ford to City: 'Drop Dead!' "

But I didn't care. I was down in the basement, looking at my boy Mike.

Mike was standing there with his arms crossed up, his head cocked to the side, and his Chuck Taylors spread about three feet apart. Told me to drop "Just Begun" by Jimmy Castor on the turntable. The music played but he kept standing there. I looked at him like he was crazy.

"I'm making this speakerbox! You interrupted me to watch you stand there like that?"

"Just wait a minute."

BAM! As soon as the drums started, Mike went nuts.

He was movin' his feet and dancin' all fast, but not like any kind of steps I'd ever seen before. Bouncing and tapping like he was doing the good foot, but Mike's moves threw in shit like I'd seen in karate flicks.

Then all of a sudden, he's popping his arm out of joint and locking it into a shape like it's broke. Whipping his leg over his head so fast, I couldn't see how he did it. Pantomiming his hands and arms like he's a robot trapped in a box.

Then he starts moving around the floor, shuffling his feet in the strangest way *ever,* sliding backward like he's walking across the surface of the moon. All the while, still popping and locking his arms and wrists and anything else he could bend.

Mike finally stops and strikes a pose, facing right at me. Arms folded up, chin down, head cocked, feet apart, daring the world to do something about it. Big, sly, easy, shit-eating grin on his face.

The whole thing couldn't have been more than ten seconds, tops.

"What the hell was that?" I couldn't believe what I'd just seen my boy do.

"I just broke on you," he said, cool as a cucumber. "And you can call me a b-boy."

Popping, locking, b-boying, and baby-rocking.

This wasn't the down-on-the-ground windmills and backspins and acrobatic stuff that people imagine when they think about "break dancing" today. Wasn't called "break dancing" at all.

This was breakin'.

This was about finding that little piece of the song where the vocals and the melody dropped out and you didn't have nothing but rhythm. And then shaking your ass on it.

Suddenly, in the summer of 1974, there were all these new dance styles to do whenever the music dropped. Crews began springing up all over the place and you'd see b-boys breakin' all over the Bronx.

What's more, everyone had their own thing. Cats like Keith and Kevin, a.k.a. "The Nigga Twins," were known because they had a smooth syncopated style, kinda like Fred Astaire but with their own brand of funk and soul. They dressed alike and timed their moves perfectly. Sister Boo showed how the girls could get down just like the fellas.

There were crews like Boston Road and Edenwald, and some cats, like Bumpy Faced Melvin, Flippin' Mike, Profile, and Mean Gene, were simply the best around.

Breakin'.

This new style of dancing spoke for itself and changed as the music changed. But it also spoke to the music we were playing. The funkier the music got over the years, the wilder the dancing got, and the wilder the dancing got, the more the music spoke directly to the b-boy.

Herman Kelly.

Kool and the Gang.

Seventh Wonder.

Those guys were challenging break-boys to show what they were made of.

Back at the clubhouse, E-Z Mike was still down on the cardboard, staring up at me like he just invented sex.

"Where'd you learn that?" I asked.

"Me and my boys at school got us a crew. Got so many fresh moves, nobody wants to battle us."

Breaking was all about battling, just like graffiti. Breakin' on somebody was the attitude you had to have if you called yourself a b-boy. You had to be ready to battle at the drop of a hat, whether you were on the street, in a park, or at a jam, and you had to be on your shit if you dared to compete.

That's what Mike's finishing pose was all about—putting your enemy's challenge out there and talking with your skills. A flagrant pose said, *Beat that*. Clowning on another guy's moves by mimicking his style was like saying *You suck*. Battling got mean. Sometimes, you'd humiliate a guy so bad, he'd come back at you with a pool cue or a broomstick. Some breakers would even front-flip and land on your ass, and flipping would instantly turn a party into a barroom brawl.

I was a brawler in my heart, but not in my lungs. I wanted to be a boxer like my uncle and my dad, but I didn't have the breath or the stamina for it. I could go a round or two with quick fists and accuracy to match anybody my size, but asthma kept me from making it in the long run.

Maybe breaking was my way to put the rhythmic skills I had inside my body to the test. Maybe breaking was the fight I was looking for.

"How can I be down?" I asked Mike.

"Sorry, man," he replied, still grinning. "You gotta go get your own crew."

I told him that was some bullshit, but he insisted. Besides, he didn't make the rules; the crew's the crew.

Me and Mike went to different schools and sometimes ran in different crowds because of it.

"But I'll show you some moves if you want," he said.

I said yes.

A week later, I had a few moves down, so I hooked up with three dudes I knew over in the South Bronx. One of the kids, named Bumpy Faced Melvin, had a loose dance posse, a dance crew. I wanted to be down, so Melvin held an audition.

Melvin asked me, "What's your specialty?"

"Backflips," I told him. It was bullshit, of course, but I figured I could learn later.

Walter, one of the other two dudes in the crew, spoke up: "Yeah, I can do those. What else can you do?"

"What we really need is someone who can do the electrician," said another kid named Marcus. "Is that you?"

"Uh, yeah! Sure." Again, bullshit, but whatever. I had a feeling I could dance better than I could spray-paint.

They voted on it, and by a narrow margin the dance posse let me in on a trial basis.

We hadn't actually practiced, but Melvin thought we could compete, so we went out looking for action. We made it as far as Third Avenue, where we found another crew, four deep, just like us. When Melvin said one of the other dude's mamas danced like a silverback gorilla, it was on.

Right off the bat, I knew the other crew was tight. Those guys had a practiced routine and knew when to tap out. Plus, they had a home turf advantage—which meant a cheering section. Most of all, each dude was better than the last and the final dancer did a front flip into the splits, then gave Melvin the bird.

Our turn. Melvin led off, but it was obvious he wasn't as good as he said he was. When he tried a one-armed handstand on the curb and messed it up, everyone started booing.

The crew went downhill from there. Marcus and Walter weren't even as good as Melvin. What's more, the more the crowd booed, the more Melvin and the guys fucked up.

Finally, it was my turn. I knew if I did something cool, we could at least turn the tables on the crowd, so I tried my special backflip . . .

Even though I'd never done one before. Mike had told me the trick was to throw your neck back when you jumped.

Except I forgot.

So I stalled out midair and landed on my spine, dead-smack on the curb.

SPLAT!

The crowd went *"Ooooob!"*

I went *"Oowww!"*

The sad truth was that the crew sucked . . . and I had a big goose egg in the middle of my back to prove it.

To add insult to injury, on the way back to Third Avenue, Melvin pulled me aside.

"Uh, Flash? Me and the guys voted and, um . . ."

I was out.

The crew couldn't roll with somebody who didn't throw backflips.

I was hurt, but it was a blessing in disguise. The South Bronx vibe—the beats, the heat, the graffiti, the flippin' and flyin' and breakin'—was all around me.

Even if I wasn't supposed to dance . . .

Somehow I'd make my move.

Somehow I'd make my mark.

HOO-TAAAH!

It's the next day. My back is still sore.

The graffiti scene's blowing up. The b-boy shit's wild. I wanna be on the inside, but I'm not.

Instead I'm up on the roof, flying a kite. Normally, my kites are what I need to let off steam, but it's no use today.

Like building my electronics, kite flying is my thing. Like boxing and breaking, kites are another way to scrap with other kids in my neighborhood. Kites are another way to let it all out. Wanna battle? I'm game. I make my kites myself, using the finest tissue paper, the straightest bamboo sticks for the frames; taking 'em out for test flights, then trimming the panels so I can duck and cut and juke faster. I'm always looking for new tricks to build the best battle kites, or sneakies, on my block.

My secret weapon comes from boiling up some fisherman's glue, grinding a fluorescent lightbulb into glass powder, and mixing 'em together into a sharp, viscous goo. The goo turns an ordinary string into a deadly-sharp razor-line . . . the perfect weapon to slice my enemies' kites out of the sky.

Down in the basement, I'm a geek with a soldering iron. But up on the roof, I'm a dogfighter. Shouting out when I cut my enemy's kite loose, watchin' it go off in the wind.

HOO-TAAAH!

That's what you yell. "Hoo-Taaah" gets everybody on the street to look up as the other dude's kite flies away. "Hoo-Taaah" lets everybody know you won. The whole thing's square, but man, it's a blast!

But it's not a blast today.

Today my back's sore and my head's spinning. I can get over the pain in my back, but my head's another story.

What I'm spinning on is far more important.

A few days earlier, I was riding home from school on the train, and looked up and saw two cats sitting across the aisle—Sa Sa and the Amazing Bobo, who I know from around the way. Unlike me, they were really good dancers. Bobo was hitting Sa Sa up with a play-by-play of his adventures from the night before:

"You missed it. This girl Cindy threw a birthday party over on Sedgwick Ave. Her brother's a *slammin'* DJ with a killer sound system. You woulda been all over that ass!"

"What's so special 'bout his shit?"

"It's his records. He breaks 'em up and takes those motherfuckers apart, piece by piece. My man got everybody out on the dance floor 'cause he was playing the best parts and movin' on to the next jam. Not even waiting for the first one to end. I got *mad* tired, I was bustin' so much movement!"

"He doesn't play the whole jam?"

"No, yo. Just the drums and the get-down part."

"Like on what?"

"Lotta that Culo Dancehall shit. Lotta James Brown. 'Apache' by the Incredible Bongo Band."

"Yeah, yeah! That's my jam, but they never play that shit on the radio!"

"I know, right?" Bobo said. "Know the part in the middle?"

I know exactly what Bobo's talking about. And just like he says, it's straight-up percussive beats.

"The dude's jumpin' all over the mic, sayin' we gotta ride the break, callin' us breakers and b-boys," Bobo continues. "I got this fly girl out on the floor and she's givin' me a look like she's ready to freak if I can just keep her goin'. Shiiiiiit . . . by the time the song's over, I'm back at her house, having this wild-ass orgy."

"What's this dude's name," Sa Sa asks, "the one with all the records?"

"Clive, but everybody calls him Kool Herc."

DJ Kool Herc.

After I get home, I can't stop thinking about it. Try to go up on the roof and get my head right, but it isn't working.

Suddenly, flying my kites feels like kids' stuff. Graffiti writing isn't for me. And the way my back hurts? If I never try to dance again, that's cool.

All I care about is what that DJ is doing. If he can really blow up the spot with his music, I have to see it firsthand.

Next time DJ Kool Herc plays a block party, I'm going.

GODS AND MONSTER SYSTEMS

DJ KOOL HERC

and the Herculoids

return with . . .

—THE BAD MACHINE—

!!!SURE SHOCKER!!!

With

COKE LA ROCK & DJ CLARK KENT

a birthday celebration for . . .

Wendy & Alvira!!

Saturday, May 25, 1974

CEDAR PARK REC CENTER

9:00 p.m.–???

16 to 18 ONLY!!!   ***   I.D. REQ.

Free admission

no guns—no alcoholic beverages—no drugs

The flier caught my eye.

Here was my chance.

Cedar Park was almost all the way to the Harlem River and ten blocks
north of my house. But I was prepared to crawl there if I had to. It was
late April and finally warm enough to be out all night in shirtsleeves,

What's more, the closer I got to the stage, the thicker the crowd, the hotter the action.

But I got in.

Herc had this huge Macintosh amp with these big lit-up displays. Thing must have been pushing a thousand watts per channel; it was so strong that the lights in the park would dim when the signal maxed out. The Mac fed these Gallahan subwoofers, two Shure vocal master columns covered the midrange, and a pair of huge Gallahan tweeters. High hats sizzling in the night air. It was the biggest phase of speakers I had ever seen.

Finally, there was the man himself.

Herc stood six and change. With his Afro and the butterfly collar on his AJ Lester leisure suit turned up, he looked even bigger. He was a god up there, the red and blue party lights behind him pulsing away on that big thumping beat.

On either side, he had no less than six guards—each seemed twice his size—watching his back. Making sure no one bum-rushed the stage, peeked in his record crates, or fucked with his sound system.

Herc also had a microphone.

As he faded between records, he'd toast the crowd and the Jamaican would come out in his voice. These aren't his exact words, but they went something like this:

YES-YES, Y'ALL ... HERC-HERC, Y'ALL!
Y'nevuh heard it like dis' before.

And he hit the echo chamber and shouted:

HERC-HERC-HERC-HERC-HERC-HERC-HERC ...

My head was spinning and all my circuits were on overload. If our clubhouse was a little firecracker, this was like somebody dropped a nuke on the Bronx.

I knew some of the music from my sisters' collections: James Brown's "Hot Pants," "Clap Your Hands Stomp Your Feet," and "Give It Up Turn It Loose." "Rock Steady" by Aretha Franklin. My man even played the theme from *Shaft in Africa*—I just saw that movie with Paulette the other week! How the hell did he get his hands on the record so fast?

But some of his music, I'd never heard before. Baby Huey's "Listen to Me." Still, they were just as slammin' as the ones I knew. And every time he played one of those mystery jams, I remember thinking: *What other songs are out there I don't know? And where the hell do I get 'em?*

Then Herc played "Apache."

When he dropped the needle on that magical jam at the end of the night, the whole place went nuts. Like the finale of a fireworks show, all the b-boys in the crowd pulled out the stops and gave it everything they had.

That's how it went until six in the morning. No cops breaking it up, no gang fights turning it loose; just everybody doing their thing, having fun, and riding the beat.

Grooving in euphoria.

But while everybody else danced the night away, I hung back in the cut, watching Herc spin his records, listening to him say his toasts and rock the crowd. Trying to understand how he chose his records.

How he knew what to play.

When he knew to play it.

By the end of the party, my whole universe had shrunk down to one single thing:

I can do that.

Part Two

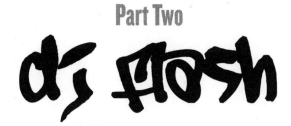

DISARRAY IN UNISON

So many questions.

Walking home from Cedar Park the next morning, here's what was running through my brain: Herc had such lovely, incredible music. How did he know what songs to play? Did he have 'em picked out before he started playing? How did he locate the get-down part of the song? Could he see that break part of the song on the vinyl? Where did he find all his jams?

How can I figure this stuff out for myself?

It was like Herc had a sixth sense for where one song reached out and a magic ear for the next perfect hook. But as monumental as Herc's insight was, there was something that bothered me about his style. He didn't care about keeping the actual beat locked in tight; he didn't make the switch from one song to the next in a clean cut that matched the beats, bars, and phrases of the two jams. He just mashed one song on top of the other.

That bothered me. I kept thinking that there had to be a more scientific method.

How? How? How?

I was tired as hell and my head was already spun with all the questions. I was thinking so hard, my thoughts eventually became white noise— loud enough that I had to cover my ears to stop the ringing.

When it died down, I took my hands away and everything was quiet. Then, as the world came back, the first thing I heard was a Transit Authority hard hat the next block down, busting up concrete. Running a jackhammer in no particular rhythm: *Chuh-chuh-chuh! Chuh-chuh-chuh-chuh-chuh-chuh! Chuh-chuh!*

Disarray.

Across the street, a kid—couldn't have been more than eight—was banging on a fire hydrant with a brick. Trying to get the cap off in the morning heat.

Ta-ta-TA-tA-TA-TA-ta-ta-TA-Ta-tA ...

Disarray in unison.

But then an alarm started ringing out.

Ring! Ring! Ring! Ring!

Finally, a beat!

First, the kid got with the program—started whacking that hydrant to the alarm. Alternating back and forth.

Ring ...TA ...Ring ...TA ...Ring ...TA ...Ring ...TA!

Don't know whether he knew what he was doing, but I was hearing it. Before I knew it, the hard hat with the jackhammer picked up on the beat and started laying into a rhythm too.

Chuh-chuh-chuh-chuh-chuh! Chuh-chuh-chuh-chuh-chuh! Chuh-chuh-chuh-chuh-chuh! Chuh-chuh-chuh-chuh-chuh!

The kid got the hydrant open and somebody turned the alarm off, but the jackhammer stayed on the beat.

Right on time.

Array in unison.

It hit me: whatever Herc was doing, he wasn't doing it on time. One song dropped out, but it wasn't on the right beat with the next one. He would pick up the needle and drop it on the vinyl—first on one turntable and then on the next—taking a chance that he would land on the break.

He was just changing the volume on two records.

I thought back to the night before. Sometimes he would get lucky and have the sync right, but other times, he'd go from a slower record—say, at 90 beats a minute—to a faster one that was bouncing at 110.

But some of these dancers now were really good—they were doing their moves *on time.* They needed to keep it going.

They needed a DJ to *extend time, and percussively rearrange the beat.*

If you looked at the crowd in that moment between the songs, everybody fell off the beat for a few seconds. They'd get back on it again, but in those few seconds you could see the energy and the magic start to fade from the crowd.

So many questions.

Never mind that I didn't have good speakers or strong amplification.
Forget that I only owned one turntable.
Don't even talk about a mixer or all the ideas running through my brain about time and beats and rhythm and unity.
I still had almost nothing to play.
If I dug around the basement for records, I might have found ten outdated jams. Last night, I had tried to keep track of how many different records Herc played, and lost count at a hundred.
B-boys and girls didn't want to hear straight four-on-the-floor dance beats and boring rhythms. They wanted music they didn't recognize but could break on anyway.
But they needed something tight.
They went with what Herc was doing because they hadn't heard anything different ...
But I had.
I had the start of a whole other vision. It was raw, but it was real. And it was right there, pumping inside my brain.

Thumping inside my heart.

TAKING IT TO THE PARK: FLASH'S UNIVERSAL DJ RULE NUMBER TWO

The park was the natural step up. It was where everybody went when the weather was nice. It was where all the girls could be found. It was also where more people were gonna hear me do my thing.

After testing this DJ style in a park down the block from my house on Brown's Place, the plan was to go even bigger. That meant the Mott Haven Projects Park on 142nd and Willis, near the Patterson Housing Projects. Mike said it was usually crowded enough that people would show up to see what was going on, especially if there was a circle of b-boys going at it. I rounded up my crew—Mike, OJ, Monkey George, and Truman—and we loaded up the shopping carts with equipment, records, and lights, and we headed over to the park.

The whole area around 144th and Third Avenue in the Bronx was already tough, and the projects made it tougher, but those towers were straight-up dangerous—they belonged to the Black Spades. This was no green-trees-and-grassy-lawns kind of place; Mott Haven projects was little more than a couple basketball courts and twenty-foot chain-link fencing.

For a minute, I thought it was just gonna be a bunch of kids like us, wanting to dance to some music and have a good time.

Wrong.

Sure, there were people hanging out, but the spot was crawling with bookmakers and pushers who didn't want anyone making a scene or drawing a crowd. On top of all that, the neighborhood old folks kept yelling at us to shut up.

Whether or not anybody wanted us there, I'd come to spin. I set up and was just about to start . . .

But somebody shook me first.

"Hey, bro," said this hulky dark-skinned brother. "Don't you know where you at?"

Me and my boys didn't say shit.

"What you doin' there?" he continued, eyeing my system.

Mike pumped up his chest, all tough: "We're just doing our thing. Ain't bothering you."

"I ain't bothered," he said as he started toward us, talking to Mike, Truman, OJ, and Monkey George but looking at me. "*You* bothered?"

Scary though he was, this guy didn't look like a thug or a pusher. He looked like a roughneck. Forceful. You could tell he was in charge of this neck of the neighborhood.

"No one's gonna do you for your fucked-up little system," he said with a crooked smile, "but you might get jacked for your records."

"Who?" said Mike. *"You?"*

"Be easy, young brother," he cooed. "I ain't no trouble."

Before I knew it, he was next to the cart, looking through my jams. He didn't ask, but this dude was huge—I wasn't about to stop him. When he found my copy of *The Payback* LP, though, his smile lit his face up for real.

"My man!" he said, to both the Godfather of Soul and to me.

I didn't know it, but I had just met Tiny, chief of the Casanovas, a crew comprised of ex-gang members of the Black Spades.

The Casanovas held Mott Haven down. Numbers, dust, or anything else illegal; you had to go through the Casanovas to get the green light. Tiny was giving me the green light to play records in the park. But not before he gave me and my sound system the twice-over.

"Your shit looks raggedy," Tiny chuckled. "Like you built it yourself. That what you did?"

"Yup," I said. I was polite and I was nervous, but I looked him dead in the eye when I spoke.

Tiny smiled again. As he handed the James Brown record back to me, I found the best break on the album to kick it off.

Tiny nodded at me as his head started bobbing, and he did a little dance move.

He sized me up and said, "You got some shine on you, young man."

Then he made a hand signal to the pack of Casanovas holding down the far end of the basketball court that meant "don't fuck with these guys."

And then Tiny walked away without another word. The whole thing was a little scary, but nobody ever fucked with us at Mott Haven Park after that. In fact, Tiny and I became really close.

I switched out JB and dropped on "Apache." It hadn't taken long, but thanks to DJ Kool Herc, "Apache" had become the biggest jam in the Bronx. I didn't know which was crazier; that everybody was grooving to "Apache" or that a DJ had the power to make a song pop like that.

As the jumping drums kicked in and E-Z Mike was getting loose, some of the best b-boys in the Bronx—Flippin' Mike, Bumpy Faced Melvin, and Black Jerry—stepped up, and stepped right to my best friend.

"I seen you breakin' over at Mitchell Gym a couple weeks ago," Melvin said to him.

"Oh, word?" Mike said, thinking they were propping him up.

"Yeah," Flippin' Mike said. "You sucked."

"Oh, no the fuck you didn't," Mike shot back, and the battle was on. He started busting on Melvin and Flippin' Mike, giving them the bird with every new dance move.

As a crowd started to form, I threw on "I Can't Stop" by John Davis and the Monster Orchestra. I knew Mike liked it for battling, and as soon as he heard his jam he stepped up his game. Bumpy and Flip tried to compete, but Mike wasn't having it.

If Flippin' Mike broke with a killer move, E-Z Mike came back with something better. Then he would grab his nuts, make a face, and stick out his tongue; the hotter the battle got, the more E-Z Mike worked insult moves into his routine. And the hotter the battle got, the more I pumped up my friend's jams.

E-Z Mike finally ended his routine with a killer one-two punch—first, he faked pulling out his dick and pissing on his enemies' shoes, then he spun around and actually *farted* on Melvin. It was timed perfectly with the end of the jam. And the crowd ate it up.

Flippin' Mike and Bumpy Faced Melvin couldn't top that. Somebody pointed at E-Z Mike and shouted what everyone in the crowd was already knowing:

"THAT NIGGA WON!"

The final insult. Bumpy and Flip knew they had got their asses whupped.

Mike smiled that easy smile at me as the crowd booed 'em away ... and the smile said this victory was mine as much as it was his.

I could feel it too—the energy between us. He was the ear and I was the voice—him as the audience and me as the DJ. But he was speaking to me too. By selecting the music and playing it right, I was pumping him up. The better he danced, the more he gave the energy back to me. It went back and forth like that, and as it did, it got bigger and bigger.

I looked at the crowd—the bond wasn't just between E-Z Mike and me—and they were feeling it too ... just like they felt the power of "Apache" every time they heard it.

The bond was between all of us. And I was the one creating it.

FLASH'S UNIVERSAL DJ RULE NUMBER TWO:
DJ's got the power.

TOUGH AS A ROSE

Y ou stay away from those Casanovas, young man," she said.

She was Miss Rose.

We'd been playing every day in the park, and the summer of 1974 was in full swing. The crowds were starting to get bigger every day I played.

Herc's name and his mighty speakers echoed all across the Bronx. If he threw a party, everybody went. If he dogged a jam, everybody requested it when I played. I might not have been at Herc's level—no other DJ was—but folks were starting to talk about this South Bronx neighborhood kid spinning good dance records on a bad sound system. Word was out: "Flash is cool. Leave him be."

But word had finally gotten around to Miss Rose. And now Miss Rose was getting around to me.

"Stay away from the Casanovas," she repeated. "They're nothing but trouble."

If the Casanovas were tough ex-gang members, then Miss Rose and them only had one thing in common—the tough part.

Back then, Miss Rose was probably in her forties, but she seemed older. Older because she didn't tolerate nonsense from anybody. Older because everyone listened to what she had to say. Older because people went to her with their problems—Miss Rose could get things done.

Miss Rose was also one of those ladies who took care of everybody else's kids as well as her own. She ran an after-school center, knew all the local politicians, and had the pull of a block association captain. And she did all of it from a run-down little storefront across the street from the park.

"Are you that DJ Flash that all the kids are talking about?" Miss Rose asked.

"Yes, ma'am."

"That the name your mama gave you?"

"No. But that's what she calls me."

Miss Rose laughed. People didn't usually talk back to her.

"Well then. I guess it's good enough for me. But you listen up, Flash. You ever need anything—anything at all—you come to *me*. I don't wanna see you get involved with that gang or crew stuff. You hear me?"

"Yes, ma'am."

"For starters, let me get you an extension cord," she said. "The police come by here and see you messing with the power, they're gonna beat your ass. That is, if you don't get electrocuted first."

Miss Rose was referring to something that had made me half-famous in the neighborhood: I'd break open a faceplate on a lightpole and, thanks to what I'd learned at vocational school, I could split the wires, step the power down, and make it all work.

From that point on, whenever Miss Rose was around, we didn't have to jack into nothing. If anybody hassled us, she scared 'em off. Nobody disrespected her.

That was Miss Rose. She was good people. After the Casanovas, she was the reason I could play that park.

She could even pull a lot of the stuff the Casanovas couldn't. When one of the pushers tried to kick us off his dust spot, Miss Rose told him to go find another one. When old people in the towers complained about the noise, it was Miss Rose who talked to 'em. And when the cops came by, they knew we were cool because Miss Rose told 'em so.

But Miss Rose couldn't do anything about my beat-up junk. And in the mid-seventies in my world, there was no substitute for a premier P.A. system. Something to make the ground shake. Something to make the beat vibrate in your soul. Something to make yourself heard.

The Casanovas could do something about my beat-up junk. Tiny was definitely making things happen behind the scenes.

One thing was clear—I needed two turntables and some big-ass speakers, not just my one decent turntable and some piece of crap I found in a backyard.

I needed professional equipment if I wanted to really rock the Bronx.

And I did.

I sure as hell did.

"NOW YOU GOT SOME SHIT"

By fall of 1974 I started to experiment with getting the beats in unison—playing my jams *on time*.

I wasn't there yet, but I knew if I could tweak the speed of the beats, I could do a whole lot more than the average DJ. Doing it better than the average DJ meant I could distinguish myself and even outdo Herc—he was still the man to beat. But to tweak the speed of the beats, I had to have turntables with pitch adjustments. And be it ever so humble, my stuff was still junk.

One day I was at the park, doing what I could with what I had, playing "Hyperbolicsyllabicsesquedalymistic" by Isaac Hayes. All of a sudden, Duck came over to where I was set up. He took one look at my system and flashed a crooked smile.

"Watch your shit," he said. "Stick-up niggas robbed the sound system outta the Hunts Point Palace last night."

Duck went on to say how they got all the booze, busted the safe open, and stole all the tables and chairs . . . but all I heard was that they got the sound system. I knew that sound system by reputation and I'd be lying if I said I hadn't fantasized about what I could do with some of that stuff.

A little while later, a Ford LTD station wagon pulled up to the curb, near where I was set up.

"Hey, Flash!" the passenger yelled. "You stay over on Fox Street, right?"

I didn't know them, but they knew me . . . and they knew where I lived.

"We got something for you. Meet us up that way in an hour."

Sixty minutes later, me and two thugs were in the Faille Street basement, staring at the sound system from the Hunts Point Palace.

"This shit's for you," said Thug Number One.

I still hadn't outgrown all of my geekiness, but I knew a hustle when I saw one.

"What I gotta do?" I asked.

"Everybody know you ain't got shit," said Thug Number Two. "Everybody know you need shit. Now you got some shit."

It was good stuff too: two Thorens TD-125C turntables—the best you can buy—with gimbaled counterweights on the back of the arms that made 'em look like something from *Star Trek*, a twelve-channel Bozak rotary mixer, and a two-channel BGW power amp, 1250 watts a side. And only one big-ass speaker. I wished they had both speakers, but I was happy with one.

"Somebody wanted you to have it," the other one said.

"Who?" I asked.

"It don't matter. All that matters is that you keep the park bangin'."

I didn't find out until later it was Duck.

I felt like there was something fishy about taking the stuff. But suddenly, I had better gear. Don't like admitting it, but I didn't care where from.

Now I could tweak the pitch to match the beats.

Now I could turn the sound up loud. *Real* loud. So loud I'd be blowing out my speaker before the volume was all the way up. And with my new mixer, I could fade between two turntables . . . *big* improvement.

I packed everything up, returned to the park.

On the way, I was thinking:

Things are looking up.

My gear was looking good.

But something was still missing.

Something big.

Without something big, I'd stay small.

And believe me, small was not my style.

FLASH'S UNIVERSAL DJ RULE NUMBER THREE

FLASH'S UNIVERSAL DJ RULE NUMBER THREE:
Without a big library, a DJ is dead.

At this point, I needed records.

Just like I dug through the Bronx for old stereo equipment, I started digging for beats.

What little money I got for school and clothes, I started spending on music. No matter where I was—high up in Harlem or over on Southern Boulevard or the Grand Concourse—I'd be at every record store I passed, rooting through funk, soul, jazz, and disco bins. If I couldn't make it to real record stores, I'd scour every Salvation Army, thrift store, and mom-and-pop grocery I could find. Back in the day, most stores had a few records for sale behind the counter. The pickings were slim, but it was the seventies—the golden age of funk and soul—and even little stashes could turn out sweet nuggets.

If I knew the group, I could usually decide whether there were good breaks on a record. If I didn't, it presented a new challenge: deciding whether a record was any good just by looking at the album cover with the plastic still on it.

Some groups made it easy, thanks to the artwork on the covers—take the Ohio Players and Funkadelic, for example. Other times I had no idea what I was buying. As a result, I had to have two crates—one for good joints and one for stiffs. A stiff was a joint that looked like it had some potential, but ended up being jive.

That meant sometimes I chose the records and sometimes the records chose me. Sometimes I came upon something great and sometimes I didn't, but finding something great was always a crazy high.

If finding something great was a crazy high, I was about to hit the jackpot.

Downstairs Records in the subway arcade on the corner of 42nd Street and Sixth Ave. If the beats were at Downstairs Records, then so was I. Soon as I walked through the door, I knew I was on to something killer. Never mind the place was tiny; there were a million records in a million different places.

Records in bins.

Records in racks.

Records in stacks.

Records on shelves.

Records on counters.

Records in boxes and crates.

Records hanging from the ceiling.

Records displayed up against the walls.

Everywhere I turned, nothing but vinyl.

Everywhere I turned, there was something cool I couldn't get in the Bronx—white boy music like the Steve Miller Band and Spooky Tooth, Jeff Beck and Steely Dan ... talk about righteous beats! Crazy beats from the Philippines and India with sounds I didn't know human beings could make. Oldies by the thousands that took me straight back to Dewey Avenue with my sisters Violet and Carmetta chasing me around the house. Whole albums of nothing but sound effects! Modern jazz like no record Bra had ever played.

Something would happen when I picked up these jams; something I could feel in my fingertips, something coming from the record itself.

Magic!

Gold on wax!

Million-dollar breaks and beats!
Hoo-Taaah!

To me, it was the gold rush of 1975:

Shirley Ellis—"The Clapping Song"
The Isley Brothers—"If You Wanna Get into Something"
Mandrill—"Fencewalk"
Herman Kelly—"Let's Dance to the Drummer's Beat"
Booker T & the M.G.'s—"Melting Pot"
Bobby Knight—"Sex"
Dynamic Corvettes–"Funky Music Is the Thing"
Dennis Coffey—"Scorpio"
Trouble Funk—"Pump Me Up"
Charles Wright—"Express Yourself"
Jeannie Reynolds—"Fruit Song"
Tom Scott—"Sneakin' in the Back"
Cymande—"Bra"

Some of 'em were straight dance records and some of 'em just had cool and sweet sounds, but every one of those records was special. Every one was new and different and personal. When I found something few others knew existed, it became *my* song.

FLASH'S UNIVERSAL DJ RULE NUMBER THREE-AND-A-HALF:
No one else can play it if no one else knows what it is.

Herc had his own private stash of songs. Other DJs coming up on the scene like Hollywood and Clark Kent and Charlie Chase did too. If I wanted to compete, I had to play music nobody knew and nobody else had.

Got me even more obsessed. Like a junkie running down a fix, I'd come running back to Faille Street—sometimes with Mike and Truman and OJ carrying as many records as me—and throw on one jam after the other.

Digging for gold.

Looking for secret beats.

Falling in love with the music all over again.

Tuning my ear for bouncing basslines and lethal drums. Stand-out vocal shrieks and phrases. Talking guitars and get-out-the-way horns. If the beats made my head nod, my knees bend, and my backbone slip as I stood over the record player, I knew I had something good.

A jam didn't even have to make me wanna dance. Sometimes, I'd hear a little piece of something and it would get a hold of me, even if there was no easy rhythm or groove. Maybe just an odd sound or a few bars of something special.

Something that caught my ear.

Something that played with my emotions.

Something that spoke to what I was feeling.

Something that I could use to express myself to the crowds that were continuing to gather every time I brought out my gear.

I even started looking for specific musicians 'cause I knew they could play. Once I found somebody with chops, I wouldn't stop digging until I had everything they'd ever cut.

Take the J.B.'s for example: Every single guy in the band was bad, but Clyde Stubblefield was the baddest. First time I ever heard "Funky Drummer," I started looking for his name on anything I could find. If Clyde played on a Lawrence Welk record, I bought it.

Same was true with Arthur Jenkins. Steve Gadd. Ziggy Modeliste. James Gadson and Al Jackson Jr. Any bassline laid down by Chuck Rainey or the amazing Bootsy Collins was most definitely in my crates.

Then there was Barry White.

I loved everything Barry did. How could he balance black funk with beautiful, soaring strings? Didn't make any sense that the two things should go together like that, but there it was.

Barry and the rest of those cats knew what they were doing. They knew how to get the funk and the stink and the groove and the fire out of your soul and put it in your ass.

They knew how to make you move.

They spoke my language.

Didn't matter whether they were playing pop, rock, jazz, blues, punk, funk, classical, opera, disco, or R&B. To me, it was all the same. It may not have sounded that way, but I knew that when a song—or even just a *piece* of a song—got that feeling going, I could cook with it. I could expand my musical palette.

I could create.

Problem was, though, how do you create when your mean green is short and your gig hours are long?

GIFT FROM GOD

My ear was improving but my ends weren't. In early 1975, I needed money.

Needed money for records.

Needed money to graduate from high school.

Needed money for something else that was about to drop in my lap.

By then, Penny and Carmetta had gone upside my head too many times for me to keep stealing their LPs. Violet had gotten married a few months back and taken her collection, as well as her stereo, with her. That meant I had to buy my own stuff. I didn't have the money for the speakers I wanted, so I invested in music instead.

That meant picking up more hours at my Crantex job and fast. In addition to the weekends, I started going into Manhattan to work after school. I missed hanging out with Mike and Truman and OJ and Monkey George, but I did what I had to do.

The job was easy in that all I had to do was round up sample fabric swatches, get an address, and jump the train. But it was hard because everybody wanted their stuff yesterday or sooner, not to mention I had to lug a lot of junk around.

Any time I started to get pissed off about it, though, I thought about my pay. Got to the point where I had it figured out right down to the delivery: one trip door-to-door equaled fifty cents. I'd think to myself, *I made two seventy-five today, so I can get the new Curtis Mayfield, the new Sergio Mendes, and the new Headhunters albums, if I can find 'em on the cheap.*

But there was another reason I needed to make money. It came in the form of a shock.

Paulette Dawson was pregnant.

Girls had become a big part of my life. The more I played, the more they came around. The more they came around, the more I noticed. The more I noticed, the more I liked what I saw.

We were in the Faille Street basement when she told me. I didn't know what to think. Mom always told us that children were gifts from God; that she was glad for each and every one of hers.

"Don't worry," I said. "I'm gonna do right by you. By both of you."

But that didn't mean that I was gonna stop the music.

I might have thought about how my own father hadn't been much of a father.

Might have thought about the awesome responsibility that comes with being a parent.

Might have thought about a lot of things.

Wish I had.

Wish I had taken the time to figure out how to do everything.

Wish I'd had the maturity for all that.

But in 1975, I was just eighteen. I was just a kid having a kid.

Besides, I couldn't stop the beat even if I wanted to.

Couldn't stop the beat any more than I could stop my own heart. It wouldn't go away and I couldn't avoid it.

There it was on the sidewalk in front of Fox Street.

There it was in the basement on Faille.

There it was in the park.

There it was at Downstairs Records.

There it was in the little pieces of rhythm and melody I was collecting.

But there it was in the questions too:

What am I gonna do with it?

How am I gonna keep the beat with two turntables and a damn mixer?

I saw how all the different breaks in the music could form a groove. A groove that got the crowd moving. A groove that lasted all day and all night.

I had a feeling I could take it further than Herc; that I could answer questions he wasn't thinking to ask.

But I still couldn't figure out how.

Besides, thinking wasn't gonna make me a DJ. I had to do something about it.

The truth was I still wasn't making enough on the Crantex tip. I'd graduated from vocational school by then and had some extra hours, so I got a second job. The building I worked in had a lot of clothing designers. They all knew I was going uptown to where they had their stuff made. When they told me I could make an extra dollar a pop delivering garment patterns and samples on the down low, I took it.

God works in mysterious ways. Sometimes it's through side work. That side work helped me with the next step. Helped me answer another question.

Riding the train with those samples and patterns, I could see how all the different little pieces made up a jacket or a blouse or a suit. You had to cut each panel with precision or the whole thing wouldn't be even. Overlapping wasn't good enough.

Everything had to stitch together to make a seamless groove. It was just like when I was building a kite or an amp—the pieces had to fit. Had to fit precisely.

The beats, the beats, the beats!

How do I match 'em up?
How do I smooth 'em out?
How do I put 'em together?
How do I make 'em last?

"THE GLUE, BABY, YOU GOTTA FIND THAT GLUE"

Get outta my house and take your damn beats with you!"

Mom was pissed for a lotta reasons.

She was pissed because of Paulette.

She was pissed 'cause I hardly ever slept.

She was pissed 'cause if I was awake, I was spinning records.

She was pissed 'cause if I was awake...and if I was spinning records...then everybody else was awake too.

So Mom got fed up and kicked me out.

Mom got even more pissed off when I moved in with Paulette Dawson over on 181st Street and Burnside, but by then it was none of her business. In reality, it was the best thing for everybody; our daughter Tawanna had just been born, and for a short while just after my eighteenth birthday, me and Paulette and the baby were a family.

The problem was that I still had to spin. Paulette's apartment wasn't the spot for me to make noise, especially with the baby, but we were able to find another apartment with a tiny basement on Brown's Place. Thanks to a small trapdoor in the back of a closet, I had a little hole in the ground that would accommodate a dozen people and all the beats I could serve.

It wasn't all I had. I had ambition. I had ideas. I had gear. I had records. But there *was* one thing I didn't have—the most important thing of all . . .

The right technique.

Blending records.

Mixing them.

Cutting the beats together in exact syncopation and planning out my DJ sets like a chess game. These were the next steps to my progression as a DJ.

By now, I'd go see Herc every chance I got, which sometimes was two nights a week, especially since by now he had taken his shows inside to a couple clubs in the West Bronx to escape the cold nights.

As for his skills, I continued to pay close attention to what I saw him do. I still had issues with the lack of precision, but I was noticing patterns and rhythms to how Herc connected the dots between his songs. Sure, he had his personal jams and crowd-pleasers that made everybody go apeshit, but I could tell that in his heart he wasn't about the individual songs.

To Herc, a DJ set was one continuous piece of music.

My man was composing something. And if he was a composer, that went for me too. I went home and reexamined my records; how did Bob James connect to James Brown? Would Mongo Santamaria work with the Meters? I'd hear a piece of one song and a piece of another and would imagine the two pieces playing over each other. Or one right after another—*on time*.

But there was a big difference between thinking and doing.

Just like with the kites, I needed a glue that was gonna hold everything together.

"The glue, baby, you gotta find that glue!"

When I tried to explain myself to E-Z Mike, down there in the sweatbox, that's what he said.

The question remained: *How?*

I knew I wanted a continuous groove. One made up of all these reorganized pieces of songs I'd found.

Had to get 'em in unison.

"I have to extend time."

"Man, how the hell you gonna do that?" Mike responded, and to be honest, I didn't have an answer for him. "What's it mean to extend time in the first place?"

We were grooving down in the sweatbox one day. I was messing with a Billy Cobham drumbeat from a record called "A Funky Kind of Thing." Problem was, I liked only about five seconds of the jam before the other musicians kicked in and ruined the break.

So I threw it on and showed him one little piece of the record that I wanted.

"Oh, I get it," Mike exclaimed. "You wanna stretch it out and make it last."

"Yes," I said, "but there's more to it than that."

Using two copies of the same record—one to play and one to cue up while the other was playing—was the easy part. That was the thing that Herc had already figured out. That's what made him so popular. The hard part—the part that Herc *hadn't* already figured out—was playing them right on time.

Playing them right *exactly* on the one.

I explained it to Mike again: "I need to stop the record on the left and start the record on the right at a precise moment in time so that you, the listener, can't tell where one stops and the next one starts."

After a long pause, Mike said, "You want to keep the beat."

"Exactly!" I told him.

I could spot the part of the drumbeat I wanted just by looking at where it was on the record. If I held it up to the light, I saw rings. The shiniest rings were where the fewest musicians were playing. I knew this just by watching the needle travel through the groove.

The break. That's what Herc called it.

It was also where I knew to put the needle down—now I knew roughly where the drumbeat was.

But "roughly" wasn't gonna cut it. "Roughly" was good enough for Herc, but it wasn't good enough for me.

I wanted to *cut.*

Which got me back to my original problem: I didn't know where the song was gonna be playing when I let the record spin.

Trial and error time.

I started to play the first copy of "A Funky Kind of Thing." Listened for where the break ended. As soon as I heard the last drum hit—BAM!—I threw the fader over to the second duplicate copy.

But the second record wasn't playing where I needed it to be. So I wound both records back and tried again while E-Z Mike watched . . .

and watched . . .

and watched . . .

and watched.

I tried counting out the beats, but that didn't work. I tried starting the second turntable in the right place, but I always got it wrong.

I tried everything.

I tried starting the record player with the needle in the groove, but the speed wouldn't be right. I tried dropping the needle down on the spinning record, but it sounded horrible.

No wonder Herc wasn't trying this shit.

Nothing worked. But I had something stuck in my head and I couldn't get it out. So I kept trying.

Finally, I found a way to start the first record with my hand physically on the vinyl itself. The platter would turn but the music wouldn't play because the needle wouldn't be traveling through the groove. However, when I took my hand off the record . . .

BAM!

The music started right where I wanted it.

It was that simple, but I had just made my first discovery.

At the same time, this was a major no-no among other DJs. You *never* touched the record with your fingers. But if touching the records was wrong, I didn't want to be right.

I finally had a way to control one record, now I needed a way to control the beats.

What if I could do this with two turntables at once?

It wasn't easy, but I kept winding the second record back and forward until I got it just right and . . .

BAM!

I threw the fader . . .

Success!

The beats matched up!

The break played twice without missing a beat!

I COULD DO THIS!!!

I was so excited, I danced around the Brown's Place sweatbox until the record stopped spinning. I looked to Mike for some love but he was asleep. He might have been my best friend, but even best friends can lose interest.

But maybe Mike had it right. After the thrill was gone, I looked at the facts: It took me three days to play two songs perfectly. To get ten seconds of music *just right.*

One cut.

Ten seconds of music.

Six times a minute . . .

Sixty minutes an hour . . .

Times ten hours.

I would have to do that thirty-six hundred times to fill an all-day park jam with music the way I wanted to play it. For all the hassle it had been to get that one cut, it seemed impossible.

But I knew it could be done.

So I practiced.

And Mike slept.

And ideas started coming fast.

And I kept at it until something beautiful happened.

A new kind of birth.

A birth I'd never seen before.

The birth of a theory.

The birth tied to time.

And time tied to beats.

And beats tied to the beauty of a continuous rhythm.

Meanwhile, the tick-tock stayed steady. The groove grooved on, smooth as silk.

And suddenly, I had it. Something new. Something I called . . .

THE QUIK MIX THEORY

Few days later, I knew every drumbeat on "A Funky Kind of Thing" backward, forward, and sideways. I could make that one cut with my eyes closed.

But rubbing the records back and forth had beat 'em up and worn out the grooves. Those two copies of "A Funky Kind of Thing" were ruined.

Plus, I still had a lot of unanswered questions. At the top of the list, I needed to know where the intro and the outro of the break was at all times.

I needed an easy way to find exactly what I wanted to play on the record. I had to know the exact spot where the needle hit the groove and I had to have a quick way to get there—and to get back again.

Down in the sweatbox, watching the label on "A Funky Kind of Thing" go around and around, I thought I was gonna lose my mind. I knew the first drum always hit at the same spot. As soon as the label with Billy Cobham's name was facing straight up on the spindle, BAM! There it was. If I wound the record back, BAM! There it was again, in the exact same spot.

What if I marked that spot on the record?

I took a grease pencil and drew a big line on the label of the record, pointing right to the first beat in the break—now I knew exactly where

I needed the needle to hit the beat. Then I let the grease pencil trace a line around the record as the break played—now I knew exactly where the break started and ended.

Now I had a formula:

1. Flip the fader as soon as the end marker hits the needle.
2. Wind the other record back while the first one plays.
3. Wait for the break to finish.
4. BAM! Throw the fader on turntable number one and start all over again.

That's how my clock theory was born. With the label facing up, the top was twelve-noon, the bottom was six, three was to the right, and nine was to the left, which was where I placed my fingers on the record to manipulate it, once it was on the turntable. Sometimes a break would start at four, go around three times, and end at nine. Other times, the piece of sound I wanted was so short, it would start at two and wouldn't even hit six before it was over. My clock theory was blasphemous in the eyes of other DJs—actually putting your greasy fingertips on a record back in the day was the cardinal sin—but now it was like I had a roadmap to the beats. I'd never be lost again. Better yet, now I knew where I was going.

I'd gone from breaking a song apart in my head to breaking it apart on the turntable. The possibilities were endless. Being able to cue up the beats instantaneously meant more time to experiment with them. Breaks could play together. Breaks could play all alone. And just like with b-boy dancers and graffiti writing, breaks could play against each other too.

That's what I was thinking one day when E-Z Mike yanked open the trapdoor and came running down into the sweatbox with a b-boy about our age, who I didn't know.

"Flash, this is Disco Bee," he said. "Sucka thinks he can whup me in pop-lockin'. Quick, throw on a jam."

"Assembly Line" by the Commodores and "It's Just Begun" by Jimmy Castor were both killer-diller dance tunes. I'd also noticed they had similar beats per minute.

This battle gave me an idea.

I said, "Cool." Then, turning to Bee, I continued: "You're up first. Soon as you got a beat, do what you feel."

BAM! I threw on "Assembly Line."

Disco Bee began throwing elbows, shoulders, and wrists like he was knocking on every door in town. No question, he was good and he knew the song.

I could tell he was saving a big move for the break that was coming, but no way could I let Mike get dissed. So right before it dropped . . .

BAM! I threw the fader on "It's Just Begun," and just like I thought, it threw Bee.

E-Z Mike saw his chance and fought back. Busting out his own moves and doing it right.

I could see by the look in Disco Bee's eye that he felt robbed, but he couldn't accuse me of playing favorites. After all, the beat was right on time . . . just like I knew it would be.

Still, I was going to make it interesting. Soon as Mike got into his own groove, BAM! I gave it back to Bee by cutting *back* to the Commodores. He picked up on what I was doing and answered the question.

That's what mixing two songs together felt like. A question and an answer. One song would ask, the next one would respond. It wasn't just a battle between two b-boys, it was a battle between songs as well. I might have kept my eyes on Mike and Bee, but my ears were on the music and my hands on the turntables.

For the next fifteen minutes, the three of us lit up that little dark basement like *Soul Train.*

As we did it, I got the same feeling from the night I watched Herc at Cedar Park, the same feeling from my mom and dad's house parties.

It was the euphoria of the beats.

Except this was better, because I was creating it.

The more I spun, the better I got. Cutting back and forth, faster and faster. Mike would get going and BAM! I'd switch the song. Bee would get the upper hand and BAM! I'd cut again. It got to the point where nobody could hear where one song ended and the next one began, not even me. But it didn't matter. We were in the groove.

And I was plugged in. I had a natural sense of where the two records were spinning. At one point, "Assembly Line" fell off the beat for a split second and I dog-paddled the record backwards . . .

Spin back!

Then I punched it forward right on the break . . .

Punch phase!

Zuka-Zuka! It sounded like a beat! But the drummer didn't play it, I did! And the rhythm was still on time!

I was making these beats myself!

Zuka-Zuka!

Zuka-Zuka!

Zuka-Zuka-Zuka-Zuka-Zuka-Zuka-Zuka!

I let "Assembly Line" play.

Took my hands off the console.

Felt like I was plugged into my own system, electricity running through my veins, chargin' up that old, crazy high.

The high I'd been searching for my whole life.

The high I got from the euphoric union between the music, the audience, and me. The satisfaction of melding all my techniques together into something greater than the sum of the parts: the Clock Theory; the Spin Back; the Punch Phase; the Back Door; the Front Door; and the Double Back. This new thing—cutting—*Zuka-Zuka!* All this added up to the Quik Mix Theory. There it was, the culmination of all my creations.

By now, Bee and Mike were just standing there, staring.

Mike marveled: *"What the fuck were you just doin'?"*

"I don't know," I said. And God help me, it was the truth.

Maybe I'm not creating this thing after all. Maybe it's something working through me.

Mom talked about being moved by the spirits. Maybe that's what this was—God or Jehovah; Jesus, Buddha, Allah, or Jah.

Because it sure wasn't Flash.

When I woke the next morning, I knew that there was no going back. No obstacles ahead.

From here on, it was up, up, up.

DOWN, DOWN, DOWN

So excited.

Gotta share this thing I've found with the rest of the world. Otherwise, I'm gonna go crazy. If I can get people to hear what I hear, they'll feel what I feel.

By 1975, I knew how all the pieces fit together. I knew how I was gonna rock a party. When b-boys and party people heard my new style, they'd lose their motherfuckin' minds.

I'd been practicing since the session with Mike and Bee, and I was improving by the day. What's more, those guys had been talking me up:

"There's this really good DJ named Flash and he's playing records like nobody else."

Herc was still the man. Herc was the DJ who would shut a whole weekend down. If he was throwing a party somewhere in the Bronx on a Saturday night, nobody dared to compete.

I still wasn't famous like DJ Kool Herc, but the word was out on me. Now it was time to showcase my discoveries in public.

I had come up with all my new methods and techniques and I had perfected them. I had felt the energy in the room that day with Mike and

Bee. I was sure everybody who heard my new style would feel the same thing.

I was wrong.

The day came in early July. Disco Bee borrowed his mother's car. Mike, Truman, and OJ helped me break down my gear. We loaded everything in the back and drove twenty blocks north to 23 Park at 166th and Tinton Avenue, which was four times the size of Mott Haven, and ripe for an all-day jam.

Had everything set up by noon and ready by one.

By two, there was a crowd of about five hundred people. All kinds of folks. Hardheads and thugs. Moms and pops. Kids of all ages. Hundreds of girls. Miss Rose. Even Mom and my sisters.

By three, Mike told me, "Yo man, it's now or never."

I needed an introduction, so he stepped up to the mic: "Uh, ladies and gentlemen . . . boys and girls . . ."

Nothing. The crowd was quiet.

For a second, my heart stopped beating: *C'mon, Mike!*

"FREAK-FREAK, Y'ALL! TO THE BEAT, Y'ALL! EVERYBODY GIVE IT UP FOR MY BOY DJ FLASH!"

It wasn't much of a mic check, but heads turned toward the DJ table and suddenly all eyes were on me.

Now or never, just like Mike said.

Zuka-Zuka-Zuka-Zuka-Zuka!

I punched in the opening beats of "Apache." And I proceeded to play it my way.

I extended the horns . . .

I repeated the breaks . . .

I paused between the organs and the guitars . . .

I rearranged the structure of that song at will . . .

And I never lost the beat.

Then I quik-mixed five more songs. Back to back to back to back to back.

And nobody got it.

A thousand people stood there listening to my Quik Mix Theory and they didn't make a peep. When I finished I couldn't believe it:

There were no b-boys getting down in a circle.
Nobody was bumping and grinding.
Nobody was wilding out.

Nobody got it!

Maybe my speakers weren't loud enough. Maybe the people didn't recognize the jams. Maybe they weren't in the mood. Maybe they just didn't understand.

Whatever it was, you could have heard a pin drop in that park, and my stomach was starting to twist. I looked over and saw Miss Rose, Penny, Lilly, and Mom. They could tell I was crushed. I could see them hurting for me, but there was nothing they could do.

And as my whole world was falling apart, I thought I saw my father.

Dad.

He had become a ghost in my life by 1975. Violet kept in touch and would give us the news: how he had a new family, new kids, a new job, new girlfriend. The couple times I'd seen him, we talked a little bit, but it didn't last long. A few months earlier, I'd asked him for a loan to throw a party, but he'd said no.

"Go get a job … a *real* job," he told me before hanging up the phone.

Now he was out by the edge of the crowd on the other side of the fence. Staring back at me, watching as my dream fell on deaf ears.

Worst of all, he was laughing.

I told you not to mess with the motherfuckin' music!

I looked twice.

Dad wasn't really there.

But it felt real enough.

I wasn't any good to spin after that. Miss Rose was coming my way, but I had nothing to say to her or anybody else. I was gonna be sick.

As soon as I was out of the park and out of sight, I puked up my lunch.

Then I ran all the way back to Brown's Place, crawled into the sweatbox, and cried for days.

IN MY HEAD AND IN MY HEART

Days turned into weeks.

At times I'd run up to see my little baby girl, Tawanna. She melted my heart. Loved holding her and hearing her coo. I adored her to pieces, but even the joy of a newborn didn't beat back my blues.

I tried to work out the feelings in my head and in my heart, but I couldn't do it. Tried to make sense of why people didn't get my style, but I had no answers.

Kept seeing my father's face laughing at me.

Kept hearing rumors that I was the DJ who scratched records and ruined 'em. People hated me for no reason.

In my head, I was a failure.

In reality, people just didn't get it. But I couldn't understand why.

Wanted 'em to get it so bad.

Please get it. PLEASE be excited like me.

I just wanted to be understood. Instead, people screwed up their faces and said:

"Why is he doing that?"

"Why is he making those noises?"

"Why is he repeating that part of the jam?"

"Why is he moving the record in the wrong direction?"

And most important, to anybody who didn't know any better, "Why's he putting his hands all over the vinyl?"

Far as I was concerned, I was done. During those weeks, I didn't play my turntables once.

Didn't want to spin.

Didn't want to shop for records.

Didn't wanna go to work, even with Paulette yelling and the baby crying.

Instead of getting out of my funk, I got out of Paulette's house.

Couldn't move in with Mike.

Couldn't move in with Mom.

Couldn't move in with Truman or OJ or any of my sisters.

So I moved in with Mean Gene Livingston.

Gene was the neighborhood bully and a real bastard, but he was also a DJ, so at least we had that in common. His mom, Mrs. Livingston, was cool too, and she didn't mind the DJ gear. In fact, Mrs. Livingston was like a second mom to me. She didn't care what kind of noise we made or when.

Problem was, I didn't give a fuck about DJing ever again.

But one more time, God had better plans for me. They say that when the student is ready, the teacher appears.

It was a Thursday, a couple weeks after the disaster in 23 Park. I was coming home from work, walking past Miss Rose's place on 143rd. I was almost past the window when I heard her voice:

"Flash! Get in here."

Even if I was depressed, I still didn't dare say no to Miss Rose.

"I haven't seen you in the park recently. Everything okay?"

"Yeah," I lied.

"I don't believe you. What are you doing this Saturday afternoon?"

"I dunno," I said. "Probably nothing."

"Then be over in the park at three."

"Why?"

"Don't you worry about why, young man," she shot back. "You just be there."

"Butsy" around four or five. *(Courtesy of Regina "Penny" Saddler)*

My parents, Regina "Gina" Johnson Saddler and Joseph Saddler, in the 1950s.
(Courtesy of Regina "Penny" Saddler)

My older sister "Penny" in the 1970s. *(Courtesy of Regina "Penny" Saddler)*

My older sister Violet in the early 1970s. *(Courtesy of Regina "Penny" Saddler)*

Dad with my little sister Lilly in the 1970s. *(Courtesy of Regina "Penny" Saddler)*

My sister Carmetta and her son, my nephew Shante, in the 1970s. *(Courtesy of Regina "Penny" Saddler)*

Before a show at Virginia State College in the early 1980s. *(Courtesy of Mark Green)*

"Cowboy" at Virginia State College. *(Courtesy of Mark Green)*

My best friend, EZ Mike, at Disco Fever in the early 1980s.
(Courtesy of Regina "Penny" Saddler)

Grandmaster Flash and the Furious Five. The original Sugarhill Records publicity still. Back row, left to right: Eddie Morris, a.k.a. "Mr. Ness" and, later, "Scorpio"; Keith Wiggins, a.k.a. "Cowboy"; Guy Williams, a.k.a. "Rahiem"; Melvin Glover, a.k.a. "Melle Mel"; Center: Me, Joseph Saddler, a.k.a. "Grandmaster Flash"; Front, left: Danny Glover, a.k.a. "Kid Creole." *(Echoes Archive / Redferns / Retna Ltd.)*

2007
Rock and Roll Hall of Fame

INDUCTEES
Grandmaster Flash and the Furious Five
R.E.M.
The Ronettes
Patti Smith
Van Halen

A SPECIAL TRIBUTE TO
Ahmet M. Ertegun

The night it all became official. The program from the Rock and Roll Hall of Fame induction ceremony for Grandmaster Flash and the Furious Five, March 12, 2007. Hip hop is part of the canon forever.
(From the collection of Bill Adler/eyejammies)

At the Rock and Roll Hall of Fame,
March 12, 2007. Doing what I do best!
(Robert Caplin / The New York Times / *Redux)*

With my kids and my nephew in 2003. Back row, left to right: Joseph "JoJo" Saddler, Jr.; Kareem Saddler; Me, holding Christina Jester; Tawanna Dawson. Middle row, left to right: Lalonnie Dawson, Keith Saddler. Front row: My nephew Kendall Grant. *(Courtesy of Joseph Saddler)*

As I was leaving, Miss Rose added one more thing: "Bring your sound system."

Saturday rolled around and I did what Miss Rose asked. I called up Mike and Bee, loaded up the shopping carts, and left out for Mott Haven.

Going over there, my head was still spinning.

If people didn't get my style, why was I doing it?

If they didn't care, why should I?

I didn't have time to answer those questions, because at the corner of 140th and Willis, the ground started shaking. Just like the night with Herc.

I was three whole blocks away.

WHUMP!

WHUMP!

WHUMP!

As we rolled in, I saw a big crowd and another big array of speakers, just like Herc's. I also saw a big dude with a big Afro and sharp threads.

Except it *wasn't* Herc.

The dude sitting behind the console was older. And he didn't have a posse of guards, he had a bevy of lovely ladies—at least two to a side. They'd hand him his records and shake their moneymakers for the crowd while they were digging through his crates.

WHUMP!

WHUMP!

WHUMP!

He wasn't even playing my kind of music; this guy was spinning Earth, Wind & Fire, the Emotions, and Gloria Gaynor's "I Will Survive," but I didn't care—he was rockin' the crowd. Plus, I also noticed his style and I liked it. He wasn't cutting like me; he was blending records smoothly, slow fades and clean transitions.

He also had this incredible GLI 7000 mixer. It allowed him to listen to the record that wasn't playing, via headphones, just like my peek-a-boo system. Most of all, he was keeping the beat rock steady, and I instantly respected him for that.

Miss Rose came up and said, "That's Pete DJ Jones. He wants to meet you."

This guy wanted to meet me? He was a grown-up; a professional DJ. I was a kid.

"Why does he wanna meet me?" I asked.

"I told him about you."

"What'd you tell him?"

"Quit asking so many questions," Miss Rose scolded. "Go over and introduce yourself."

A couple minutes later, I was looking up at a six-foot-eight-inch gentle giant. Turned out Pete Jones was a big disco DJ on the club circuit. One night, he'd be downtown at Nell Gwynn's, the next night he'd be up at Harlem World, the following night he'd be playing out at the Factory in Queens—this cat got around.

"You must be Flash," Pete said with a hint of a Southern accent, never taking his hands off his turntables. "It's a pleasure to meet you."

Speaking of his hands, they were huge, but you could tell by the way he laid 'em on his equipment that he had a soft touch. Giant or not, Pete used his hands like a heart surgeon.

"Miss Rose tells me you're a good DJ," he said.

"I'd be better with a system like that," I said, pointing at his monstrous speakers.

"System ain't where it's at," Pete chuckled. "Keeping the beat. *That's* where it's at."

This cat was a trip! If I'd asked anybody else, they would have said a DJ's only as good as his system . . . but not Pete.

"Let's see what you got," he said.

My man motioned to one of the ladies, Miss Becky DJ Jones, to take over. I couldn't believe it when she stepped up to the turntables and started spinning just as smooth as him. He saw me looking.

"Girls been noticing you on the turntables yet?"

I shrugged no.

"They will," he continued. "Lotta perks to being a DJ."

Maybe. But I was still intimidated, especially when we got to my homemade speakers and crummy old turntables. Regardless, Pete genuinely wanted to hear me spin, especially after he flipped through my records and liked what he saw. I was still scared, though, and he could see it. So he looked at me square and asked a simple question:

"You wanna DJ or not?"

Without waiting for an answer, Pete plugged his mic into my mixer and signaled to Miss Becky: *ALRIGHT, STOP!*

Oh shit. Now everyone's looking over here . . .

Pete continued: *"Now clap your hands, everybody! Everybody now clap your hands!"* Pete started clapping and they followed; followed with a nice, clean, easy beat.

No turning back now …

Pete continued: *"Right about now, I want y'all to give it up for the finest DJ in the South Bronx … He's one of your own … so show some love … for the KIIIIIIIIIID … FLASH!"*

Please God, just let me keep this beat.

I listened to the clapping.
Then I let my mind go and felt around for the pocket.

There. At the end of the clap. That's where I pick it up …

Soon as I slipped inside that deep soul rhythm, I dropped the needle on "Cissy Strut" by the Meters.
Right on the beat.
The six-note lick ended in a double hi-hat right after the first chorus: *DO-do-doo-do-DOO-DOO-TSS-TSS (fader, spin back) DO-do-doo-do-DOO-DOO-TSS-TSS (fader, spin back) DO-do-doo-do-DOO-DOO-TSS-TSS (fader, spin back).*
It was about as fast as I could cut between two records, rewind the turntable, and throw the fader. Tricky, yes, but I did it eight times straight. Still safely in the pocket of that beat. Then …

Zuka-Zuka-Zuka!
"… IIIIIIIIII just wanna celebrate!"
Chukka-chukka-chukka-chukka-CHONK!
"… IIIIIIIIII just wanna celebrate!"
I had swapped out the Meters for Rare Earth. And I was repeating it with a punch-phase spinback.
Pete got what I was doing. And when I looked over, there was a smile growing on his face. He had never seen my style of DJing before.
I'd been thinking about a new jam, "Seven Minutes of Funk," by the Hold On Family, and the Bob James record, "Take Me to the Mardi Gras."

They wouldn't rock a crowd by themselves—they weren't dance jams. But they might work together.

BAM! I cut Bob James in and cued up the drummer's paradiddles . . .

Then sped up the tempo so the beats would match up . . .

BAM! Dropped the horn blasts on "Seven Minutes" . . . and I married those two jams together, still holding on to the beat like it was money.

Now the crowd started to move. Black Jerry and Sister Boo formed a dance circle and people gathered around.

I punch-phased, switched to James Brown, and let it play out. Then I looked over at Pete, who was looking back at me all funny—not like I was a kid, but like I was his equal.

"Where the hell you learn that stuff?" he asked.

"It's just in my head."

"You mean you came up with all that stuff on your *own*?" he said, like he couldn't believe it.

I shrugged again. The music spoke for me better than words did.

"That's mighty impressive. You gotta get out there."

"Why bother?" I asked. "Nobody understands."

"That's why you gotta get out there."

Pete got serious and looked me dead in the eye again. "You got skills, Flash. Nobody else is doing what you just did. Keep at it and you're gonna be a star."

Me? A star?

"Learn to read the audience, Flash," he continued. "If people don't get you, you gotta find a way to make 'em understand."

I *didn't* understand, though, and he could see it. So Pete waved his arm over the crowd. "This here ain't about you. It's about a party. *I* get what you're doing. And your friends get it too. But there's three of us. And there's *three hundred* of them."

As I watched the crowd move, I started to understand.

"It's not about you, Flash," Pete said, as he pointed to the people. "It's about the energy *they* got. They give it to you . . . you give it back to them stronger. Again and again and again. That's how it works."

In that moment, everything made perfect sense.

"They just want a good time," Pete continued. "It's your job to serve it to 'em. By any means necessary. Remember that and they'll always take care of you. Forget it and you won't be worth nothing to nobody."

SLINKY SILK & SPIT SHINE

This new scene is weird, it's different, but I don't have time to reflect; I gotta spin.

I can hardly see the record on the turntable because of a gigantic mirrorball that's shining back in my face. I can hardly see the crowd in the center of the room because the dance floor lights up . . . *the shit lights up!* There's smoke machines blowing clouds and the air is thick. There's sweat and wet heat dripping off the brass railings leading up to the DJ booth . . . and I don't know if I'm really here or in the middle of a fantastic dream. I know that if I *am* dreaming, I don't wanna wake up.

One thing I know; I'm not in the Bronx.

It's late 1975, and I'm in the middle of the disco scene.

I'm in a place called Nell Gwynn's. Downtown Manhattan. It's full of beautiful people—black, white, Puerto Rican, everybody. Everybody's dressed to the nines: tight-fitting three-piece suits for the guys, slinky silk slip-dresses on the girls, spit-shined leather lace-ups, and calfskin high-heels with open toes. Frosted and blow-dried perms. Turquoise eye shadow.

These folks are slick and sexy.

They're sophisticated and fancy.

They're the most glamorous things I've ever seen. Look like they just stepped out of a movie.

I'm here 'cause Miss Rose said Pete Jones needed an opening DJ.

Pete's telling me, "Find a way to reach the crowd. Your job is to get the party started with the opening set and do it in your own style."

So I'm spinning:

Bohannon—"Let's Start the Dance"

MFSB—"The Sound of Philadelphia"

People's Choice—"Do It Any Way You Wanna"

Eddie Harris—"It's Alright Now"

B.T. Express—"I Like It"

Everybody's in love. In love with this place. In love with the scene. Hot for the sexed-up music. Sucking in the romance that's filling the air and feeding the night. Dancing to get aroused. Getting aroused to fuck.

I drop on "The Mexican" by Babe Ruth . . .

The heat rises on the dance floor.

Front and center, there's a dude in a white suit with his lady, who's wearing a Pucci dress. They take over the dance floor. He pulls her in close and runs his fingers down her arched neck . . .

I love you!

But at the last minute, she turns her head when he moves in for a kiss. Enraged, he pushes her away . . .

We're through!

And she spins on her toes all the way to the other side of the room, her dress flying up in a circle . . .

Fine!

But he pursues, the lights changing the color of his suit as he slides to his knees, gliding twenty feet across the glass-bottomed floor as Barry White sings:

"Baby, sweet baby . . ."

He holds his arms out, begging her for one more chance . . .

"What am I gonna do with you?"

And she gives in to him. I know one thing for sure, they're gonna be doing the hump tonight.

Around one in the morning, the joint's full. Pete gets on the console and plays "I Will Survive" by Gloria Gaynor, "You Sexy Thing" by Hot Chocolate, and "Disco Inferno" by the Tramps.

I watch Pete blend the jams perfectly. I watch the crowd eat it up and play out the stories of the music. I feel the power in the sexiness of those disco jams.

Disco gets that old feeling running through my muscles and nerves again. My head is spinning with the crazy, romantic fantasy of this late-night scene. Everything about it has me spinning except for one thing; the most important thing of all.

The beats.

Disco is most definitely *not* homemade. Disco DJs play the whole song. Disco DJs don't mess with the beats.

Even still, Pete's impressed: "You did alright out there, man."

He gives me seventy-five bucks and says, "Can you be up at the Stardust Ballroom in the Bronx tomorrow night? I got another gig."

A gig's a gig. And even if the disco club ain't my thing, I'm in the game.

And the game is most definitely heating up.

SWEET 19

By the end of 1975, I opened for Pete wherever he wanted and whenever I could.

Thursdays, we did a boat ride on the Circle Line. Weekends, we were in Manhattan again, at a high-roller's joint called Superstar 33 in midtown.

I still had the fever to turn the party out my way, and the South Bronx was still my place to turn it out like that. Didn't matter that it was rough and grimy compared to the disco scene I now knew. I had to get back to the parks and the street corners, the basements and the house parties. Had to get back to the bring-your-own-bag and do-it-yourself scene. Had to get back to messing with the beats. Had to get back to doing it my way.

Had to get back to what I wanted to do in the first place.

On the nights I wasn't opening for Pete, I played wherever I could set up. I'd pack the joint with sweaty bodies and loud thumping music, and fill the air with my music, my mix, and my style.

Some nights I was down in Paulette Dawson's basement. Some nights I was rocking a house party. If I didn't have a house party lined up, it meant I was rocking a gym or a rec center.

I was everywhere and people were listening.

By the end of 1975, I was spinning every night of the week.

Still, neither my system nor my reputation was as big as Herc's. Herc could draw a thousand people at two bucks a head with just the mention of his name.

I couldn't.

Herc was promoting himself. Herc was handling his business. I was playing for somebody else or playing for free.

But that was about to change.

The turning point came on a cold evening in November. Me and Disco Bee were rocking the P.S. 63 school yard up on 169th Street and Boston Road for fun and for free, and had been all afternoon. There were a hundred people dancing and hanging out, but as the sun went down, the temperature dropped and the party started to die.

So much for that jam.

I was about to call it a day when a guy about seven feet tall with very fair skin approached me and introduced himself as Ray Chandler. I heard of the Chandler family, and *nobody* in the neighborhood ever messed with the Chandlers.

I had been warned about Ray Chandler. I knew he wasn't a choirboy. But I also knew he was making moves and making money.

"Hey, Flash," he said, "why don't y'all come inside? I got an empty room here. And heat."

"Heat sounds good," I said, being noncommittal.

"So does a buck a head to get in."

"Who'd pay?" I asked.

"Everyone."

I had to stop and think. Until now, I'd been giving it away. But Ray Chandler was talking about charging heads.

Sounded right. But it also sounded wrong.

Wasn't the whole idea that these beats belonged to everyone? Weren't you s'posed to ride these beats for free? When I heard 'em for the first time, I sure as hell didn't have to pay.

At the same time, the song everybody was singing was the O'Jays' "For the Love of Money."

Bra always said, "Money talks and bullshit walks."

Besides, I had a kid to support.

"Hey!" Ray suddenly yelled to the crowd. "Y'all want to keep this party going?"

The crowd murmured, but didn't shout its enthusiasm.

"I can't hear ya!" Ray roared. "I said, how many of y'all wanna hear Flash do his *thing all ... night ... long? Inside?*"

All it took was a little promotion and the crowd was good to go.

Ray looked at me.

I looked at him.

"Cool, Ray," I said. "Let's do it."

Fast-forward a few months to New Year's Eve 1976.

My nineteenth birthday party.

I was down a flight of stairs.

Down in a dark, dank, hot, and nasty little room.

The room didn't fit more than a hundred people, packed to the rafters.

The place was far from legal.

But the place was the Black Door nightclub.

And the Black Door was ours.

The Black Door was a rocking hellhole for the b-boy scene. In about a month, it had become the hottest club in the South Bronx, thanks to Ray Chandler's word of mouth, my DJ skills, and my MC rhymes. Now b-boys and party people had a club to call their own.

By New Year's Eve 1976, I had a little club to call home.

As I dropped the needle on "Get into Something" by the Isley Brothers and "Scorpio" by Dennis Coffey, E-Z Mike and Disco Bee were right there to mix in the next two records: Dyke and the Blazers' "Let a Woman Be a Woman, Let a Man Be a Man" and Babe Ruth's "The Mexican."

By New Year's Eve 1976, I had a crew.

I quik-mixed the next record and two rival b-boy crews started battling front and center on the floor. As I upped my game, the b-boys did too. There was a circle of about forty people yelling, "Go! Go! Go! Go!" to the music. I cut my beats to their steps, and they timed their dance moves on my cut.

We were in sync. Didn't remember the names of all the crews that came to hear me spin, but they were at the Black Door every night I was. Even better than that, they all told me they didn't wanna battle to any other DJ's music.

By New Year's Eve 1976, I had fans.

At the back of the room, Tiny and four of his friends—Cletus, Football, Hootenany, and Big Man—were stomping the tar out of some poor ass-hole bootlegger named Katt, who was trying to tape my set. Week before, Katt had got a warning. Now he was getting an intense, furious, critical beatdown for ignoring it. And as loud as the music was, I could hear Katt screaming out and crying for his mama.

Two nights before, the Casanovas had kept Paulette from getting in the club; another girl I was seeing on the side named Yvonne was already there.

At one point, the Casanovas even had to confront a rival crew from Boston Road to act as my security in a hood that wasn't theirs, but when they rolled up in a flatbed truck and three dozen guys got out, there was no arguing with them.

By New Year's Eve 1976, I had an army of bodyguards.

As I cued up "Rigor Mortis" by Cameo, a flashy hood by the name of Joe Kidd got past half a dozen Casanovas, stepping up to the table with a foxy Puerto Rican girl on his arm.

"Hey, Flash!" he shouted. "What's good?"

Joe Kidd was a stick-up artist of the first degree; even the Casanovas let him alone. But tonight, he was mackin'.

"What do you need, man?" I asked him, a little irritated. "I'm right in the middle of this beat!"

"Just play me 'The Mexican,'" he said. "This is my girl Maria—she ain't Mexican but that shit's still her favorite jam!"

"I got you guys, Joe."

But instead of hitting the dance floor, Joe stood there a minute while I mixed out a Cameo jam and mixed in his song, phasing a couple guitar licks for good measure.

"How'd you do that?" he asked.

"You know how it is," I answered. "I just do."

"Ain't never heard shit like that before," Maria said.

Joe turned to Maria and said, "Nigga right there is like some kinda grand chess master. Only with records."

"For serious?" Maria asked.

"Yeah!" Joe Kidd shouted.

Then he looked at me and said the words that changed the way I saw myself for the rest of my life . . .

GRAND.
MASTER.
FLASH.

Master (n.): A person who has dominance or control of something.

That's what it said in the dictionary when I looked it up. That's what I did to the music. That's who I became known as in the clubs, at the parties, and on the street.

Grand.

Master.

Flash.

Everything I had wanted to be as a graffiti writer, everything I had wanted to be as a b-boy, I was becoming as a DJ. I'd gone from being the kid who messed up your records to Flash, who messed with the beats. You could still find somebody who didn't like me, but word was getting out: I was the nigga who drove the crowd insane.

There were DJs who hated me, but everyone wanted to emulate my quik-mixing method. Out on the streets, people started to know me like they knew Herc.

Herc was still the king of the Bronx, and he wouldn't let me forget it. Maybe he was jealous or scared, but he would try to humiliate me whenever we crossed paths. If I went to the Heevalo or the Executive Playhouse—those were the clubs he played at—he'd get on the mic and mumble:

"In order to be a real DJ, you've got to have a sound system like this ..."

SZZZZZZZZ ... Herc would crank up the treble on his sound system and cut the air with quivering high notes.

What he was really saying was: *Your little system ain't shit.*

But by then, his sound system was all he could hold over me, and he knew it.

Otherwise, why would he be so mean? Every time he disrespected me, I thought, *Why isn't he happy? I'm taking this thing he started and making it better.* Maybe like with Bra and his records, Herc didn't want anybody fucking with what was his. And just like with Bra, the more Herc reacted, the more it made me want to keep doing my thing.

The other big DJ on the come-up was Afrika Bambaataa. Bam wasn't like Herc; Bam was cool.

Bam had the best music library I've ever seen. When it came to records, nobody else could match his collection, not even close.

I'd go to a Bam joint on the East Side and he'd rock a set of jams I couldn't dream of matching. He'd throw on the Pink Panther theme, but with a drumbeat. Then he'd get black folks dancing to "Honky Tonk Woman" by the Rolling Stones. Then an Aerosmith jam. Then the Beatles. Then the Monkees. Then Grand Funk Railroad or Led Zeppelin. Then he'd play five songs in a row that would have you scratching your head, saying: *"Who the hell was that?"*

Being an ex–Black Spade, Bam always had a gang of hardheads around him to make sure his parties didn't go AWOL. The Spades weren't as thuggish as the Casanovas—Bam was into positive energy and community building—but they did what they had to do to keep the peace.

They made it hard to get to the DJ table, but when I did, Bam was always nice. Bam was the kind of cat who would loan me any record he had.

But other cats weren't so cool. In fact, most DJs would sell out their mamas to find out what I was playing, then play it to death their own damn selves. Keeping the names of my beats to myself gave me the idea for ...

Flash's recipe for foiling rival DJs who try to steal his beats:
1. Take favorite record.

2. Soak overnight in Mom's bathtub.

3. Slide label off so no one can spy name of jam.

4. Repeat steps 1–3 with some whack-ass Hare Krishna LP.

5. Glue Hare Krishna label onto favorite record.

6. Play favorite record at party. Let rival DJ spy name on label.

7. Laugh when rival DJ buys the whack-ass Hare Krishna LP.

Other guys had clown moves too—guys like Magic Mike, DJ Breakout, DJ Casanova Fly, Tony-Tone, and Charlie Chase.

The whole scene was blowing up.

I was making enough dollars that I passed my gig with Pete to LuvBug Starski and began headlining on my own. Word was out: if you wanted the best DJ in the South Bronx, you got Flash.

Every time I brought down a club, I wanted more—wanted to get the crowd higher. It was like a drug. And anything that pumped us up went in the pot.

There *was* something else. Something more. Another element to the scene that could take everybody higher.

We called it . . .

RAP!

Herc had his toasts to the crowd.

Muhammad Ali could humiliate any man alive, whether he was in the ring with Joe Frazier or on the mic with Howard Cosell.

Way back in the day, they called it "scat." I remembered some of Bra's old Cab Calloway records; *that* cat could talk some shit.

If it's one thing black folks in the ghetto know how to do, it's talk shit. Been talking shit, singing shit, chanting shit, rhyming shit, and mumbling shit since day one.

Wasn't hard to see what talking shit over a beat could do to a party. I saw what happened when Herc said his name into an echo chamber. Saw what happened when he said, "YES-YES, Y'ALL!" or "TO-THE-BEAT, Y'ALL!" Saw what happened when somebody with verbal skills got up and rocked the mic.

People paid attention.

Didn't mean *I* could talk shit, though. Never mind it was too hard to bust a rhyme and spin records all at once; words and vocal tones just weren't my game.

But there *were* cats around who could.

I hadn't forgotten Pete's words: the DJ's job was to rock the party by any means necessary. As a result, this new DJ culture that guys like Herc and Bam and I were creating was giving birth to a new form of expression that had everything to do with talking shit.

And the cats who were doing it called it MCing, which then became rap.

Herc had guys who would say little things and talk to the crowd when he was spinning. Other DJs *could* spin and rap at the same time—guys like DJ Hollywood and LuvBug Starski—even if they couldn't cut like me. But if I wanted to get bigger, the answer was simple:

I needed lyrics.

I needed a cheerleader.

I needed somebody to tell the crowd who I was.

I needed somebody who could just talk and talk and talk . . . *shit*.

Now, whenever I played, I put a mic up for anybody who thought they could do it.

Big mistake.

Every clown on the block who wanted to be cool stepped up. Each one acted like he was born to rap, but then the beat would drop and the crowd would clap and he would lose the act in a second.

ME: "Okay, you're on . . ."
THEM: "Uh-huh-huh-huh-huh . . . never mind."

NEXT . . .

ME: "What'cha got?"
THEM: "I'm the one they call nice, I'm super nice, I'm the kid so nice, they named me twice."

NEXT!

Got to the point where I could spot a clown as soon as he started rapping:

A clown mumbled.

A clown's voice was weak.

A clown's lyrical routine didn't make sense.

A clown didn't think about rocking the crowd 'cause he didn't understand—I was trying to get the party going and I needed somebody who could dig it.

I needed somebody who could bark from the gut.

I needed somebody who could spit, and I needed him quick.

I was playing P.S. 63 Park one afternoon when the crowd parted and this stocky, bowlegged guy came walking through, just like a cowboy. Before he could grab the mic, though, Jamal—a tall, skinny kid—blocked this guy and grabbed it himself.

"Step aside, Black," Jamal said. "I'm about to do this."

The Cowboy spoke in a rich voice that was as friendly as a gameshow host, but as forceful as a cop. "I'm goin' first. Lemme please have that mic." He looked Jamal dead in the eye, even though Jamal had six inches on him.

"Bitch, I'll bust your ass," Jamal said.

"Gimme the mic," said the Cowboy, still smiling. "I ain't askin' again."

BAM! The moment Jamal began to make a fist, the Cowboy threw a lightning-fast uppercut and bombed him right in his jaw. Laid Jamal out like a side of meat.

He even took the mic out of Jamal's hand as his ass went down. As the crowd howled bloody murder, the Cowboy turned to me, smiled again, and said, "Can you give me a funky-ass beat?"

I wasn't about to say no. And as soon as I cued up "Seven Minutes of Funk," the Cowboy started rapping.

Damn, this guy was good! I could see the crowd was feeling it, and so could he, so the Cowboy took it directly to 'em, and the crowd exploded!

Keith Wiggins—a.k.a. Cowboy—was the perfect mix of a hype man and a prizefighter. He rocked back and forth, bounced up and down, swayed, jumped, clapped his hands, waved his arms, and acted out his routines. Keith did whatever it took to get the crowd moving. And the crowd ate out of the palm of his hand.

KEITH: When I say ho, YOU say ho—Say HO-oo!

CROWD: Ho-oo!

KEITH: SAY HO! HO!

CROWD: HO! HO!

Could have told 'em to jump off of a bridge and they would have done it. He barked, belted, hollered, and shouted out his routines, routines he conjured up on the spot, from his guts and from his heart. He had a natural ear and a gift for making others feel the beat like he did. Talking shit was in Keith's blood.

As I played jam after jam, the rest of that afternoon, I knew. I knew that whatever records I spun, Keith would instinctively know what to say and how to say it. Best of all, I knew I had my first rapper.

Walking home that afternoon, I saw the cover of a newspaper:

VIKING SPACECRAFT LANDS ON MARS
NASA: "mission to see if life exists on other planets"

Was there really life on other planets? I knew there was a new life-form down here on Earth.

The Mic Controller.

The Master of Ceremonies.

Also known as . . .

the MC.

RIGHTEOUS KINGS

Who needs life on other planets? The rap scene here
on earth is out of this world ...

For a while, it was just me and Disco Bee on the turntables and Keith-Keith on the mic. Plenty of other cats rapped to the beat, but none of 'em had his flavor; none of 'em could get a party started like the Cowboy did.

Cowboy wasn't afraid to tell all comers that he was the man to beat. But what he really loved to do was tell stories, making 'em up on the spot, and waxing 'em with that amazing voice of his.

It was Flash on the wheels of steel and Keith Cowboy on the microphone. Nobody could rock a party as hard as we did.

Then came Creole.

Nathaniel Glover was a kid from the Morrisania section of the Bronx who went by the street name of Kid Creole. One day when I was spinning records at 23 Park, Keith was off doing his own thing, so I asked the crowd if anybody wanted to be upstanding and rap. Creole approached.

If Cowboy charged like a bull, Creole swam like a fish; he had a smooth glide to match. Even his hair—braided in tight, thin rows—looked like scales on top of his head. "Lemme flow with it, Flash," he bubbled.

So I cut up "Music, Rhythm and Harmony" by Brooklyn Bridge and told him to get into it.

And Creole let it flow:

One, two, this is for you, you, and you
Three, four, cuts galore

Like a fish, he shimmied and shook, dipped, dived, and socialized.

Like a fish, he inhaled the beats through his gills and they animated his big, round eyes and little, round face.

Rhyming on the mic was what truly brought this kid's soul to life.

Creole embodied a smooth, free style. He didn't have Cowboy's bombastic disposition and he didn't play to the crowd, but everything he said was juiced-up, oil-slicked, and beautifully improvised. I'd say, "Creole, get on the mic," and he'd run with it. He would rhyme all night if there weren't any other rappers.

If you gave him a word, Creole could flow with it for five minutes, going off like a marathon runner.

In a word, Creole was fluid.

One day he brought his little brother Melvin over to my place. I knew the kid was a decent b-boy, but was surprised to learn he could MC.

"Melvin's got skills, Flash," Creole told me. "Give him a shot! Serious— he gets heavy! He's the whole reason I write rhymes in the first place!"

I looked at the kid, but I didn't see any fight in him, not at first. He was handsome enough in a clean-cut, high-yellow way, but he didn't have the kind of face that popped out of a crowd.

And *Melvin? Oh, man*...I didn't want to be rude, but nobody was gonna give it up for MC Melvin. So after a few minutes of intense deliberation, Creole's brother got a new name.

When he stepped up to the mic, he said something like this:

My name is Melle Mel
And I rock so well
From the top of the World Trades on down to the depths of hell.

Mel charged like a bull and barked just like Cowboy...but if Cowboy's bark was like the guy at the circus, Mel's bark was like a dog. Mel *growled* out his rhymes, like if you came too close, he'd chomp off your hand and chew up the mic to get to the rest of you.

Not only that, the kid must have been paying attention in school. Mel dropped *serious* English on the crowd when he spoke. Mel told stories like Cowboy, and he could boast like Creole, but he could also get extremely creative with words, writing line after line to make you think. I'd be tripping on something he'd said, and by the time I could get my mind around it, he'd have spat out three more verses, just as clever.

On top of all that, Mel had an incredible stage presence that came to life when he rhymed. When Mel grabbed a microphone, his shoulders arched back, his muscles flexed, his chin jutted forward, and his face hardened. Melle Mel had an edge. I might have been the king of the DJ scene, but *nobody* wrote rhymes like Mel. Unfortunately, he knew it.

"Nigga, if I say we need more MCs, that's how it's gotta be," Mel barked one day when he came to the Black Door with a smooth cat in a bowler hat.

It was his homeboy, Mr. Ness. Everybody knew Ness from around the way, and while he didn't have the best rhyme skills, he had amazing personal style. From the way he dressed to the way he moved, everything this cat did was smooth.

"Fuck that noise if he can't rhyme," Cowboy said.

"Fuck *you* if you don't like it," Mel told Cowboy, and seized up like he was getting ready to swing on Cowboy. "Flash might be the grandmaster on the turntables, but I'm the grandmaster on the mic!"

"You ain't the boss of this outfit, nigga!" Cowboy shouted, as he shoved Mel back. "It's Grandmaster *Flash* . . . *and* the Furious Four MCs!"

I loved being a DJ, and I liked calling the shots, but I never wanted to be too bossy.

Almost right from the start, this was how we all got along: Mel was brash and aggressive, which sometimes led to arguments between him and Cowboy. When Rahiem joined us—a soft-spoken, pretty kid—from the troubled DJ Breakout crew, he and Ness were always going at it over girls. And Creole simply got tired of it all. Whatever chemistry we had *on*stage, my job *off*stage was to keep these five furious MCs in harmony.

Grandmaster Flash and the Furious Five.

Fights or not, Grandmaster Flash and the Furious Five MCs was a force to be dealt with when we got live. Cowboy rocked the crowd, Creole rocked the flow, Mel rocked the entire English language, Ness rocked the style, Rahiem rocked the ladies, and I rocked the turntables harder than ever.

I even developed a method of cutting to match the switch-over rapping style—Cowboy, Mel, Creole, Rahiem, and Ness shuffling rhymes between one another—and once I got a feel for their individual voices, I could mix the levels on each of their mics so that they all sounded like one continuous MC routine.

There were other DJ/MC crews, like the Cold Crush Brothers, the L Brothers, and the Funky Four, but nobody could touch us.

That meant the clubs started getting bigger. The Black Door was followed by the Dixie and the Dixie was followed by the Broadway International. People continued to talk and the lines outside the club got long. They got so long that the doors would open at eleven and *close* at twelve. If you didn't get in by then, you weren't getting in at all. But if you *did* get in, you weren't going home 'til six in the morning.

Eleven to twelve-thirty, you got b-boy hustle music. Dance jams and battle cuts. Eleven to twelve-thirty was for the b-boys and girls in the crowd. B-boys and girls went on early 'cause they couldn't be battling if they'd already been rocking steady for three hours.

One to two-thirty was prime time. Those were the hours to grab your partner—I was about to play the hottest shit in my crates: "The Bells," "Johnny the Fox," "Seven Minutes of Funk," and "I Can't Stop" by John Davis and the Monster Orchestra—the Furious were about to show you what they could do, and you were about to shake your ass for ninety minutes straight. And when you were good and ready, I'd throw on my hottest record, "Apache," which I'd save for Cowboy, signal to him, and the jam would be on:

COWBOY: Somebody say party!

CROWD: PARTY!

COWBOY: Say party!

CROWD: PARTY!

COWBOY: If ya ready to party and ya know it's a fact, I want ya say, "and ya know that!"

CROWD: AND YA KNOW THAT!

The others would join in and the guys wouldn't stop for the next hour and a half. One to two-thirty was when you got the best of me and my crew. If you could tell where one record stopped and the next one began, or where Mel handed off to Cowboy, or if Rahiem rapped the same part of the jam last night as he did tonight . . . then your ears were better than mine.

As for me, I could do anything once I was in that magical zone. I could spin around, cut with my hands behind my back, hit switches with the top of my head, kick off my shoe and throw the crossfader with my foot.

From three to four, it was time for long-play breaks like "Dance to the Drummer's Beat," "Humpin' " by the Bar-Kays, Van McCoy and "The Hustle." The good shit I'd picked up from gigging with Pete. Jams to let the party flow.

And from four until the breakadawn, we cooled it *way* out. Droppin' the slow jams. After dancing and sweating all night, who wouldn't appreciate some old-school love songs?

The Delfonics—"For the Love I Gave You"
The Moments—"Look at Me"
The Five Stairsteps—"Ooh, Baby, Baby"

When I would cut the same line over and over and over again, it got everybody in the mood and kept you there. By the time the club let out, folks was ready for love.

Yes-yes, y' all . . . by spring 1976, something big was about to break.

I WANT YOU
(BUT I WANT YOU TO
WANT ME TOO)

I want you ...
The right way ...
But I want you to want me too ...

Just something about the fragrance of this chick. Just something about the scent of my Sweet Pea.

Hot summer night. Marvin Gaye's soulful sounds are driving the beat straight into my head, my heart, and my sex.

I want you ...
But I want you to want me too ...

He's a fool for the girl in his song and I'm a fool for the one I got in my arms.

Getting high on her scent: cocoa butter and sweet perfume, and a little sweat to make it salty. Sweet Pea and I are alone together at my place. She finally agreed to go out with me. Right at this moment, the only two things in my world are the scent of her neck and the touch of her booty.

Beautifully proportioned for her rail-thin body.

Moves like honey through my hands.
Moves in waves, lapping up against me.
Coming all the way around, movin' back to mine.

But this booty didn't want any part of me six months ago.
Had to work for it.

I was playing the Dixie the night I first saw her.

I was cutting "Apache" and cutting it good. Punch-phasing some horn-stabs off a marching band record. Keeping the beat like I was delivering the mail. Rocking the place like I was supposed to do.

Usually I had my eyes on the tables—you got to know where the needle is to keep the beat—but I could play "Apache" with my eyes closed and the crowd still lost it. So I was watching the room instead.

That's when I saw her.

Wearing a satin jacket, embroidered with a name:

INTRUDERS

There were eight more jackets just like hers. The Intruders Crew. Spread out in a line; taking up space, throwing down moves. Showing the room that the floor belonged to them.

And there was that booty, in the middle of the line, doing the slap. I looked up past a slim waist and narrow frame. Past the satin jacket. Up the long, thick, glistening black hair. Past sharp features and dark velvet skin ... up-up-up ... I followed that booty up and saw her face for the first time, a face that framed her burning brown eyes.

One look inside those eyes and I knew. Had to get that girl or die trying. Had to get that girl—body, mind, and soul.

I threw out a line on the mic: "WHAT UP, Y'ALL! INTRUDERS IN THE HOUSE!" But it didn't faze her.

The name embroidered on the back of her jacket said ...

SWEET PEA

So I tried again: "THIS ONE GOES OUT TO MY MELLOW MISS SWEET PEA! GIMME A SMILE AND PUT SOME LOVE ON IT!"

Sweet Pea noticed this time. But Sweet Pea didn't give me a smile. Sweet Pea didn't give me any love. Sweet Pea stopped dancing and stomped right up to the table.

Right off the bat, she scared the shit outta me.

"I ain't some easy chick! Believe that!"

"Be easy! I didn't mean nothing!" The look she was giving me said Sweet Pea could put my ass in the dirt. But I persisted: "Can I at least know your name?"

"Nunya!" she barked.

"Nunya what?" I asked.

"Nunya Damn Business! I ain't no groupie!" Damn, this chick was tough!

"Maybe you don't know who I am," I said, trying to be cool. "I'm DJ Flash. Everybody 'round here knows I'm the best in the Bronx."

"I know who you are and I still don't care!"

What the hell was it with this girl?

I was noticing girls more than ever. Noticing 'em at my shows and on the street. Noticing how they acted buying groceries at the store. Getting high on 'em.

Noticing what I liked and what I didn't.

Some girls were quiet. Mousy. Didn't have an opinion about anything. Quiet girls were always taking a cue from someone else. Didn't mean they couldn't be wild once you got 'em in the bed, but those girls did nothing for me.

Some girls were freaks. Freaks could be fun. Freaks had pep. But you had to play that ass before it played you. Can't say I didn't love on a freak now and again, but I knew not to fall in love.

Finally, there were girls like Sweet Pea . . . man, were they rare! Lions in the female kingdom—fierce, intelligent, outspoken, and passionate. That's what made 'em sexy.

Sweet Pea was the queen of 'em all.

"I'm sorry," I said. "For real." Sweet Pea started to walk away but I had to ask again: "Hey—what's your real name?" Must have been something in my voice, 'cause she stopped. "Serious," I said. "What I gotta do to know your real name?"

"Maybe if you didn't come at me like a mack . . ."

"What you got against macks?" I asked, still fronting.

"Nothing. But you ain't no mack."

She was right. And I had nothing to say.

So she turned and walked.

And my heart sank.

But at the last minute, she spun around and said, "Maybe I don't like a mack." Then snapped her fingers, gathered her girls, and the whole crew left the club.

It didn't take any more than that; I fell for Sweet Pea like a ton of bricks.

How, though, was she looking at me?

I want you ...
But I want you to want me too ...

I wasn't the only guy I knew who had fallen for her.

"Don't even think about it," Mel told me one day soon after at rehearsal. "That's the one they call Paulette."

Another Paulette in my life? Could I handle that?

There was another category I didn't mention before. They were real girls; girls from your past with a history between you. They could be girls you'd only been with once or they could be the mother of your kids, but either way, things changed once you got that ass. Whether that girl was still around or whether she'd moved on, whether she hated your guts or whether she still had love for you, a real girl left something behind. Real girls became a part of your life, like family.

Paulette Dawson, a.k.a. "Paulette One," was a real girl. She was sexy and intelligent and a lot of other things too, but in the end she was Tawanna's mom, and she'd be that forever. We had good times together and I was always glad to be around her and the baby, but I couldn't always be around and that made life hard for us.

And because I couldn't be around, I would notice girls like Paulette Two.

I fell hard for her, and I wasn't gonna stop until Sweet Pea loved me.

I want you ...
The right way ...

I don't think I ever worked so hard for anything in my life.

"Hi, my name's Flash. Is Paulette home?"

Three weeks later, I was standing at her front door with the only thing in this world that could truly speak for me.

A record.

Cowboy, who was trying to get with one of her older sisters, had told me to talk to Paulette, but it took me three weeks to get up the nerve to do something about it.

Now I was staring at an older, even more intimidating version of Paulette. Ms. Jeffrey, Paulette's mama. "What's your real name?" she asked, as stern as Miss Rose.

"Joseph."

"How old are you?"

"Nineteen, ma'am."

"Well, um, *Joseph*?" she said, just before ... WHAM! She smacked me upside my head. Smacked me so hard, I saw stars.

"My daughter Paulette is thirteen years old. Don't you even think about trying to get fresh with her!"

Damn. That made Sweet Pea three whole years younger than she said she was. But she could have been a hundred and thirteen and I still would have been in love.

I figured I was in for a few more whacks before I got through the door, but looking inside I noticed Ms. Jeffrey's record collection.

"You like Marvin Gaye?" I asked.

"Yes, I like Marvin Gaye. I was into Marvin Gaye when you were in diapers." Now I knew where Paulette got her sass. "What you know about Marvin Gaye?"

So I showed her what I had in my hands. "I could play it for you ... if you wanted."

Just then, Paulette stepped in the room.

"What's it called?" Paulette said.

"I Want You."

Ms. Jeffrey wound up to hit me again.

"The album!" I told her. "That's what it's called!"

Paulette came to my defense. "It's okay, Mama. He's no harm."

Ms. Jeffrey didn't let up on the evil eye, but she *did* let me near her daughter.

"I want to get to know you better," I said as we grooved on Marvin's joint in the privacy of Paulette Jeffrey's room.

"That's the same shit your boy Mel says when he tries to get with me. I ain't like that."

"You still talk to him?" I had to ask.

"That's none of your business again."

Damn!

"But he ain't here right now, is he?"

Yes!

Relieved, I leaned back on the bed. Soon as my head touched the pillow, Ms. Jeffrey stormed in the room and WHAM! Smacked me again.

"Don't you be layin' up on my damn daughter's bed, either!"

Damn! Falling in love with this chick hurt like hell, but I couldn't help it. Other girls were impressed with my rep. Paulette Jeffrey didn't care. If she was interested in anyone, it wasn't Flash, it was Joseph, even if she still called me Flash.

I want you ...
The right way ...

Flash or not, if Joseph was what she wanted, Joseph is what she got. I came back to the Jeffreys' place on the regular. Never missed an invitation. Always showed up with something for Paulette. Got smacked upside the head a bunch a times, but I kept coming back. Kept liking Paulette. Kept letting her know it. She kept saying no, but I kept asking her out.

Eventually, she came to another show with her crew. Then she came to a party by herself.

And finally ...

"When are you gonna take me out?"

I want you ...
But I want you to want me too ...

I'm actually here at the place I share with Bee up on Sedgwick Avenue.
We're here.
Me ...
Sweet Pea ...
and Marvin's playing in the background ...

I wonder if this love is just a fantasy. Paulette's body is close to mine. Her mouth is hot. Her breath is in my ear. "Don't want me, Flash," she whispers. "How many times I gotta say it?"

"I already do," I breathe back. "I wanna love you."

Marvin asks if it's lonely out there ...

Sweet Pea's lips are so close ...

But then she gets serious and looks me dead in the eye. "Your ass is gonna be mine. Your ass is gonna be into something serious if you love me and I love you back. You ain't never gonna be rid of me."

Marvin tells me not to play with something that should be cherished for life.

"I ain't afraid," I tell Paulette.

It's true.

I am not afraid.

My Sweet Pea.

She's everything I've ever wanted.

Everything that's on my mind.

Body, mind, and soul.

ROLLER COASTER OF LIFE

I'm on the roller-coaster ride of my life.

The cars are coming off the track and I can't steer 'em. But shit's getting so major for our group there's no stopping the train now. This thing we've become ...

It's bigger than me.

It's bigger than Mel.

It's bigger than the rest of the guys.

Grandmaster Flash and the Furious Five MCs is a force all its own.

But it's insane too.

One day it's a lovely thing of beauty, and the next day it's a ferocious beast of burden. We're having major misunderstandings among ourselves. We battle groups like the Funky 4, the Cold Crush Brothers, Kool Moe Dee and the Treacherous Three, and we always emerge undefeatable. Another day I hear through the grapevine that everybody's gone their separate ways—my group is doomed. Then Ray Chandler tells me we're playing the Webster Ave. Police Athletic League (P.A.L.) tomorrow—we're back on. I just need to be there; he'll take care of the guys, don't worry about it. Ray will handle any friction. I show up early as usual with my DJ partners Disco Bee and E-Z Mike and set up the equipment.

Mel and the guys go on and rock the crowd with the greatest of ease.

At the end of the night, Ray gives me a hundred and twenty-five dollars and a big old smile.

Everything's cool . . .

But then Cowboy tells me he's only getting seventy-five bucks. All the guys are complaining. I'm on this ride, but it's not free anymore. There's no free beats, no free shows, no more hangin' loose, no more playing records for the love of the game. Now it's for the love of money. Only thing I know for sure is what Ray said the other day:

Nobody rides for free.

It's a roller-coaster ride with Paulette Dawson, who's just had our second baby, JoJo, a beautiful son! She keeps telling me I gotta be around for my kids, but I can't stop the music.

It's a roller-coaster ride with Paulette Jeffrey too. One day I can't believe she's my girl, she's so sweet. Next day she's cold and hostile. Worse, she's coming to the show and kicking the ass of every girl who looks at the DJ table. Then she's comin' after me.

It's just like she said; my ass *is* hers now, and everybody knows it. One night she catches one of my girlfriends—Bonita (not her real name)—by the throat. Scratches her face up so bad, Bonita needs stitches. Then Paulette comes at me in the middle of my set, screaming: "I told you not to fuck around on me, nigga!" It takes three Casanovas—Peanut, Crazy Eddie, and Little Jay—to hold her back.

Everybody's afraid of my Sweet Pea. And anybody who wants to deal with me, deals with her too. One night I see her go after a coke dealer at the Dixie with a folding chair. Flattens his ass 'cause she thinks he's trying to hook me up. Then she comes after me again.

"I see you fuckin' with the freebase, Flash, and I'll kill you faster than that shit ever will."

But it's still the ride of my life. And I'm loving every minute of it.

———

July 1976. Hot night. Me and Paulette go see *The Omen* up in Harlem. Movie's s'posed to be good, but I can't believe the line to get in. Just like one of my shows, except three times bigger. Must be a thousand people in line. Inside, there's a thousand more.

Two thousand people!

How do you get two thousand people in the same place at the same time?

"What the hell is an omen anyway?" I ask Paulette.

"Something like a sign from the future," Paulette says.

Something like this big-ass crowd.

The Omen scares everybody bad; the crowd screams every five minutes. Me, I spend the whole movie fantasizing about the crowd . . . imagining they're screaming for me.

I see the place strung up with disco balls and flashing lights, just like Nell Gwynn's. I see b-boys and scramblers all over the floor, flipping out. I see honey dips in satin jackets and Jordache jeans doing the wop, the whole night long. I see two thousand folks screaming my name: *FLASH! FLASH! FLASH!*

"Flash!" On the way out, a Nuyorican dude steps up to me. He's rockin' a Kangol hat, red Pro Keds, and a big graffiti piece painted down the side of his bellbottoms. "You the baddest DJ in the whole fuckin' world! Me and my crew came over to see you do that thing at the Ecstasy Garage the other night, homes! Shit was *caliente live*!"

Damn! I know they know my name in the Bronx, but up here in Harlem?

On the train ride home, it's all I can think about.

Ray Chandler's thinking about it too. A week later, he says: "I got something to show you. Something big."

We jump in his Cadillac and roll across the 145th St. Bridge, then up to 165th and Broadway. Makes me close my eyes until I get out of the car. When he tells me to open 'em, I can't believe what I see.

The Audubon Ballroom.

The joint where Malcolm X got shot dead.

Malcolm X, one of the biggest men in American history.

The joint is the biggest thing I have ever seen.

The joint is a block and a half long.

The joint is totally empty.

"We're gonna blow it up in here," Ray tells me as we're casing the stage. "I know we are."

Damn. This room is big.

My sound system isn't loud enough . . .

The guys ain't ready . . .

This is gonna be another fuck-up, just like 63 Park, the first time I introduced my DJ technique to Boston Road.

Or am I ready to rock this house?

At the last minute I speak up: "You sure about this? *This?*" But Ray stops me cold.

"Yeah, nigga, I'm sure. We major. We already outgrown every hall, gym, rec center, P.A.L., and community room in the Bronx. Anything else is a step down. Just gimme a month to publicize it." Then he smiles a crooked smile and says: "I'll bring the crowd and you bring the noise. We gonna get rich up in here."

Fuck your money, is what I think, but what I say is, "I just don't want to go out of this place at the end of the night like a sucker."

Ray's smile turns into a frown. "You? *You?* Don't you know who the fuck you are? Somebody else can go out like a chump. But not you."

"No fuckin' way can we get three thousand deep! Nigga, is you crazy?! Herc can't even get three thousand deep!" That's what Creole says when I tell the guys the idea.

Creole's scared.

"Shiiiiit . . . Flash could sell out Madison Square Garden if they'd rent it to his black ass," says Cowboy.

Cowboy's high.

"We can do this," Mel says.

Mel's down with the program.

". . . But we better get the same loot as you this time around."

Mel's all about the money.

Me, I'm still conflicted. I take the train uptown to the Audubon, just to stare at it. I repeat this drill five days in a row.

There's a sign on the door from the New York City Fire Department:

MAX. OCCUPANCY: 3000

Three thousand b-boys.

Three thousand gangsters.

Three thousand graffiti writers.

Three thousand DJs and MCs.

Three thousand moms...dads...sisters...brothers...best friends... girlfriends...stick-up kids...bodyguards...Pete Joneses...Miss Roses... Ray Chandlers.

Just can't get my head around that number. Just can't believe there's that many people out there that know who I am...or give a damn.

Just keep asking the same question over and over again, every time I go up there to see the ballroom:

Can I do this shit?

The date draws nearer. I can't sleep. On the fifth night, I go by E-Z Mike's house. Mike asks me what's up. I tell him I gotta go talk to a guy about some sound equipment, which is bull.

"At this time of night?" Mike says, raising an eyebrow, but pulling on his sneakers at the same time.

Thirty minutes later, we're staring at the Audubon.

"Man, I'm freezing my balls off. What the hell are we doing here?" Mike says.

I explain the situation. Then I ask, "You think I can do this?"

My pal Mike looks over at me and smiles that easy smile. It's the smile that makes me believe, even when I don't believe in myself.

"Only one way to find out," he says.

Mike's my best friend.

I trust Mike.

But I still can't sleep.

———

September 2, 1976. 5:00 P.M.

Me and Mike and Bee show up at the Audubon with the sound system. We got the Gladiator—this monster amp we've rented from these Jamaican dudes. The Gladiator takes three people to carry—but I'm trippin' it's not gonna be loud enough. Even with the 'Fridgerators—these giant black plywood iceboxes with a quad-phase of eighteen-inch subwoofers that are so big—I'm still worried.

If we rig the speakers strategically, maybe we got a chance.

By six, the Gladiator and the Fridges are rigged.

I fire it up.

The sound bounces all over the room like a Ping-Pong ball. I pray it'll sound better once the joint's full.

I set up my crates. Make sure I got all the right jams. Around seven there's a big bang that sounds like a gunshot. The next thing we know there's black soot all over. The transformer's blown. Mike and I look at each other. He grabs one side of the Gladiator and I grab the other side and we race down a long flight of steps. We jump in the car and drive off to Gun Hill Road in the Bronx and beg the Jamaican dude who built it to fix it. And fix it quick.

After he's done, we race back and forth in between traffic, running lights and dodging cars. We get back to the Audubon by nine and it's still a ghost town.

Mel, Cowboy, and the guys are there and they're practicing a new routine—something Scorp cooked up just for tonight. Got it choreographed like the Four Tops and everything.

Rhyming like righteous poets and slinging words like jugglers at the circus on the very top of their game.

I also got something new. Something I came up with when I couldn't sleep.

A new way to cut without cueing. It's based on sight recognition and needle drops. It's hard and I don't always get it right. But I can cut twice as fast when I do it.

Grandmaster ... cut faster!

———

11:00 P.M. The doors open.

There's only three hundred souls waiting outside. They barely take up the space in front of the stage.

Fuck.

What were we thinking?

I break out. I can't handle failure. Not again. I tell Kool DJ AJ to turn on his system and I head for the door.

Outside, there's a few people milling around, but it's no mob scene. I run. Fast as I can.

Gotta get away from this big, giant mistake.

I run east along 172nd and St. Nick. It isn't safe at this time of night, but I don't care.

Gotta escape.

I find a bench and look across the river, toward the Bronx. Toward home. Toward where I came from.

I think about the money it's costing to rent that place. Two thousand dollars up front and another thousand at the end of the night. Three hundred people at five dollars a head doesn't even cover the front end.

No money for me.

No money for the guys.

No money for the Casanova crew, my security detail.

No money for Ray.

And everybody's gonna take it out on my ass. Gonna be playing the Black Door for free for the rest of my damn life ... if I'm lucky.

Ain't that a bitch.

The more I think about it, the sicker I get. The sicker I get, the less I care if I ever spin another record again.

What am I doing?

How did I get here?

What kind of life is this?

Gradually, Pete Jones's words start running through my head.

Keep at it and you're gonna be a star.

I run back to the Audubon even faster than I ran away.

1:00 A.M.

I get back and I can't believe what I see. Two blocks from the front door and the line's across the street. It stretches all the way around the block to the corner of 165th and Broadway and then up to 166th.

And these are the people *outside* the place!

Cars are double- and triple-parked and I take a look at some of the license plates. Massachusetts. Florida. Delaware. North Carolina.

I look up and see Tiny. He pulls me through the doors. As he hustles me backstage, I hear the size of the crowd in the main room before I see it.

Ain't three hundred people now . . .

I peek out from the wings.

The joint is jam-packed. *Three. Thousand. Strong.*

Kool DJ AJ is still pumping up the crowd, but as soon as he sees me, he gives me a look—*These folks are here to see you.*

I take the stage. E-Z Mike and Disco Bee follow behind me. The crowd starts yelling. One at a time, the Furious come out and the crowd gets louder and louder.

The guys are waiting. They have the same expression on their faces.

I see E-Z Mike. He smiles.

I give the house manager a nod. He hits the lights and the stage goes dark. I hear Cowboy's voice first and it goes something like this . . .

COWBOY: *The pulsating, inflating, disco-shaking, heartbreaking . . .*

SCORPIO: *The man that's able . . .*

RAHIEM: *On the turntable . . .*

CREOLE: *Creator of disaster . . .*

COWBOY: *The grandmaster . . .*

MEL: *LADIES AND GENTLEMEN . . . THE GREATEST DJ IN THE WOOORRRRRLD . . .*

GRAND!

MASTER!!

FLASH!!!

BOOM!!!

The lights come up! The room explodes! People screaming! Feet stomping! Walls shaking! The floor feels like it's undulating, moving, bending. Everything's going up and down. For a moment, I'm sure the floor's caving in, the pillars are coming down, and we're all falling straight into the subway tunnels!

The white noise floods over me again.
My senses drown out.
I fall into a trance.
And all I see is faces in the crowd.
Penny . . .
Pete . . .
Lilly . . .
Paulette One . . .
Paulette Two . . .
Some cat I remember from Gompers . . .
Herc maybe . . .
Dad . . . again . . . could it really be?
The faces nod up and down . . .
In slow motion . . .
Bouncing to the beats . . .
All eyes on me . . .
Slowly, the sound comes back . . .

Grandmaster!

                             Zuka-Zuka

Cut faster!

                             Zuka-Zuka

Grandmaster!

                             Zuka-Zuka

Cut faster!

                             ZUKA-Zuka

It's not just the guys saying it now . . .
Everybody's saying it!
Three thousand voices!

Young, old, hip, square, uptown, and downtown. I even notice white people in the audience saying it!

Everybody's keeping the beat. And I've been cutting and phasing the whole time ...

It's that euphoric union!

Feels like my nerves are gonna blow right out of my skin and I'm gonna blow the beat. Gonna trip on my own emotions and take everybody out of the moment.

But it doesn't happen.

My hand's on the vinyl. No need to pick up the arm off the turntable. I'm in full control. I keep the beat on time by spinning the records in a counterclockwise direction coming back to the top of the break. I'm rubbin'. Cuttin'. I'm doin' the zuka-zuka and the crowd's going wild. Me and the MCs connect like basketball players doin' no-look passes. Everyone knows where they need to be and what they need to do. As a group we are totally untouchable.

The ride doesn't stop for four more hours.

It's a high I have no words to explain. If I take every show I've played, every girl I've laid, and every DJ style I've made and multiply 'em all by a million, I still can't come close to explaining how I feel in this moment.

This life is like
A rollercoaster, baby ...
I love this life ...

Part Three

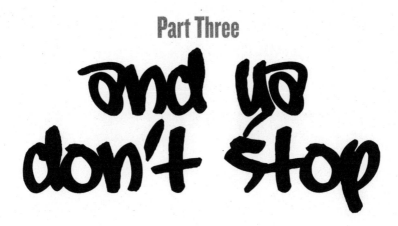

Industry rule number 4080 . . .
Record company people are shay-deeeee

—*A Tribe Called Quest*

THE GOOD QUEEN

As soon as that cream-colored Rolls pulled up out front of the club, word was out she was here.

Sylvia Robinson.

Sylvia Robinson's in the house.

Sylvia Robinson, the good queen of rap has arrived.

Sylvia Robinson, owner of Sugar Hill Records, hip hop's most prominent label.

It's 1980. New decade. New era.

Four years since that crazy night at the Audubon Ballroom.

Four years since reaching the top.

Four years of battling to stay there.

Four years of riding this roller coaster.

Four years of arguments, fights, big money, bigger sound systems, more babies, crazy women, hot new jams, and a whole lot more. Through it all, I set my watch by Tuesday nights. Thanks to my man Bug, the head DJ here at Disco Fever, Terrible Tuesdays are my nights on the turntables at the hottest club in the Bronx.

What Studio 54 is to the folks downtown, Disco Fever is to us, uptown.

Disco Fever's not just for the locals anymore, though. Pimps and pushers get down right next to white doctors and lawyers on the dance floor. Japanese businessmen and punk rockers fight to order drinks at the bar, while the bump and grind here is all about rails and flake.

Everybody's here at Disco Fever to see the same thing.

Hip hop.

This thing we been doing for years now. It's old to us but new to the rest of the world.

Hip hop's this new thing exploding all over the radio, thanks to the Good Queen.

Since the mid-seventies, me and the Furious and a hundred other guys have been established in the Bronx. We've been rhyming and cutting and rocking live shows all night and all day.

Guys like Herc and Bam.

Guys like Cold Crush, Funky Four, and the Fantastic Freaks.

Chief rocker Busy Bee.

DJ LuvBug Starski.

We *are* hip hop. It's ours. We brought it to life. Me and the Five even cut a record with a cat up in Harlem named Bobby Robinson. Has a record store. Calls his label the same thing as the shop:

ENJOY RECORDS
"Superappin'"
(E. Morris, R. Wiggins, N. Glover, M. Glover, T. Williams, B. Robinson)
GRANDMASTER FLASH
and the FURIOUS FIVE

The song is "Superappin'" on Enjoy Records. The song is hot and whenever I lay it on the crowd at the Fever, they love it. But the public doesn't know "Superappin'" like they know "Rapper's Delight." When I lay "Rapper's Delight" on 'em, you'd think it was Christmas. Ain't seen people react to a song like that since I heard "Apache" for the first time.

But "Rapper's Delight" ain't no "Apache."

They know "Rapper's Delight" because they hear it on the radio. They hear it on the radio because of the Queen.

A few months ago somebody laid it on me too. Me and Cowboy were in the VIP at the Fever. I hear somebody rapping downstairs. Cowboy hears it too. I look at him. He looks at me. We're both thinking the same thing: *"Who the hell is that?"*

The shit sounded familiar. At least the words did. But the voices weren't anybody we knew, and we knew everybody in the game. We go running downstairs and it ain't no live rappers, it's a 12-inch record! Who the hell made this song?

Before I know it, "Rapper's Delight" is on the radio every time I turn it on . . . for months and months.

Back to that night at Disco Fever. The Queen's got a court. Twenty deep. Some of 'em are security guards, clearing the way to the bar, some of 'em are just looking good . . . and the Queen's right smack-dab in the middle.

Sylvia's entourage hits the bar and pushes everybody out of the way. It's rough-and-tumble, but by the time she gets there, she glides right up without a hitch. The bottles pop and the Moët pours.

Then she looks right up at me in the DJ booth.

Makes eye contact.

Flashes me a million-dollar smile. Waves her bejeweled hand, then mouths the words:

"Hi, Flash!"

Sylvia Robinson knows my name.

I know who she is—she had a hit called "Pillow Talk" back in the day—but how does she know me?

Meanwhile, I'm in the booth cuttin' up the jams on the ones and twos. The floor is rockin'. Hands in the air. Folks are yellin'.

I throw on "Good Times" by the one and only Chic.

Then I throw on her jam.

Her jam.

"Rapper's Delight."

It's the reason she's the Queen. Even if I'm not feeling it, "Rapper's Delight" is a monster hit.

For a second, I think about dropping the needle on "Good Times" again, instead of "Rapper's Delight." "Rapper's Delight" sounds exactly like "Good Times."

For a second, I think about playing a tape I got of Grandmaster Caz rapping with the Cold Crush Brothers. There's bad blood on the streets about where Big Bank Hank of the Sugar Hill Gang got all the rhymes he used on "Rapper's Delight."

Before I can do anything, Sal Abbatiello, the son of the guy who owns the Fever, pushes into the DJ booth. He's holdin' a framed gold record that's even shinier than the diamonds on the Queen's fingers.

The label on the gold disc says "Rapper's Delight." It was an award given to Disco Fever for contributing to the success of the song.

"Flash!" he shouts. "Throw the song on or they won't let me keep this thing!"

People simply call it "the song."

That's how hot it is.

Sal says, "Throw on the song. I want to introduce you to Sylvia."

I shake her firm, diamond-laden hand. She's intense. I can feel an energy transferring from her to me. When I let go, I'm slightly nervous. I just met the Queen of record-making hip hop. I go back to the turntables in the DJ booth, shaken and in awe.

Seven the next morning. I'm in the cab going home from the club. I roll past the Webster Ave. P.A.L. A crew of b-boys is out on the playground, cardboard on the pavement, busting their moves and blasting a jam out of a two-ton boom box.

I can't help but notice the jam on the box is "Dance to the Drummer's Beat" by Herman Kelly and Life.

"KING OF THE RADIO WAVES"

Sylvia Robinson and "Rapper's Delight" aren't the only things got me spinning. If life was like a roller coaster back in the Audubon days, now it's like a rocket ship to Mars.

Paulette One's pregnant again.
So's Jean, a beautiful woman I also love.
But they're friends.
And I'm the daddy both times.
Plus, Paulette Two found out and kicked me out of her place.
Again.

Ray Chandler's pissed off.
Thinks I'm dissin' him.
Thinks I'm leaving him behind.
Thinks I'm forgetting who put me up.
Keeps threatening me.

Mom's not doing so hot.
Havin' mental problems again.
Sisters are on me to help out.
I'd like to, but I haven't got the time.

I have to deal with infighting among the Furious Five.

Everybody wants more of the cut.

Everybody wants to be number one.

Everybody hates everybody.

But everybody's excited about Sylvia Robinson.

I called her yesterday and she invited me and the guys out to the studio. Said it's across the George Washington Bridge, into New Jersey. Someplace called Englewood. Talked about it like it was Shangri-la.

Says she's got a recording studio, game room, swimming pool, and good times. Says I gotta come see the studio to believe it.

When I tell the guys, they want me to make the call, right there on the spot. Especially Mel.

"We gotta get with this lady, Flash. We gotta get with her now. Not to-morrow, not next week ... now!"

Ness's right there at his side. "If that cornball shit 'Rapper's Delight' can sell a million records, we can sell ten million records just reading the funnies."

Even Cowboy agrees. "Gotta get out there, Flash. Gotta get paid."

Gotta get out there.

Everybody wants to be a recording artist now. It's not enough just to rap or be a DJ.

But we already *got* a record.

We got Bobby. He's the man in Harlem who helped us cut "Superappin'."

But Bobby can't get us on the radio.

I ask a few people I know about Sylvia Robinson. They say she's cool. After all, she's the Good Queen.

Only my sister Penny tells me to watch my back. "All kinds of mother-fuckers gonna start comin' at you. But all they wanna do is steal what's already yours. Ain't nothin' but a bunch of culture-vultures."

But then the guys come back at me. "We voted," they say. "We wanna call this lady."

Guess I'm calling Sylvia Robinson.

Sylvia invites us to the studio in New Jersey. Says we should come out that way tomorrow morning. I say we don't have a ride. The Good Queen says we should take the bus.

Me and Rahiem are the only ones who can make it.

Takes a hell of a long bus ride to get there.

I feel like I'm on Diff'rent Strokes.

Me and Rahiem.

Arnold and Willis.

No way I'm making this trip without a car in the future ...

Then I see the studio.

It's big. It's brand new. Got a big sign out front with big gold letters:

SUGAR HILL RECORDS

There must be half a dozen fresh cars in the lot.

Rolls-Royce.

Mercedes-Benz.

Ferrari.

Rahiem whistles when he sees that.

And there's Sylvia. The Good Queen's got her arms out, big smile on her face. Standing at the front door like she's been waiting for us the whole time.

Sylvia introduces us to all kinds of people. Accountants, secretaries, engineers, marketing dudes, booking agents, the guys in the house band, everybody. We even meet the janitor. When she shows us the recording studio, it's on.

Holy shit ...

My man Bobby up in Harlem doesn't have anything like this. This is state of the art. The recording gear's so complicated it's scary, until one of the engineers breaks it all down to me. Could probably even build this stuff myself.

"You like what you see, Flash?" Sylvia asks.

"It's a thing, I'll most definitely give you that." I'm excited but trying to keep it to myself.

A tall man wearing a black suit and a hard face enters the room.

"My husband, Joe Robinson," Sylvia says. "Honey, this is the DJ I was telling you about."

She's the Queen. He's the King. Which one's running the show?

"I hear you're the king," Joe says, almost reading my mind, "the king of the streets. This is where we're going to make you the king of the radio waves too."

That mean they want to sign us?

"We got a guy up in Harlem." It's out of my mouth before I even think about what I'm saying.

"I know," Sylvia says, "Bobby Robinson over at Enjoy. We're good friends from way back."

How the hell does she know our business?

"I love Bobby," she continues, "but he can't take you where we can."

"If you have a contract with him," Joe says, "we'll take care of all that."

Sylvia finishes for him: "The important thing is that *we* start working together ASAP."

Doesn't feel right, this bum-rush . . .

But I like what I see:

The cars . . .

The studio . . .

The clout . . .

Me and Rahiem, we gotta talk to the guys about this. "No offense," I start saying, "but—"

There it is.

That smile again.

Givin' me the creeps like I just pissed this lady off.

"Guys," she says, "here's the deal. In the Bronx, everyone knows who you are. They know you, they love you, and they'd wait all night in the pouring rain to hear y'all do your thing. But in the real world, nobody knows you from a can of paint."

"One hit record can change all of that," says Joe.

"If that's what you want, we can take you there," Sylvia continues. "But the radio waves aren't going to wait for you, me, or anyone else. If you and the Furious Five need to wait on this, then we need to find someone who's ready to move."

Then she smiles again. "But if you're ready, then together we can all go for the ride of our lives."

I look at Rahiem.

Rahiem looks at me.

I say, *"What now?"*

BITING RHYMES

Can't sleep.

Can't sleep even if I tried.

Can't sleep 'cause I can't understand something.

Can't understand what Sylvia's pitching us.

Can't understand how if she wants us so bad, she'll buy out our record contract, but she's offering *us*—the recording artists—less cash than Bobby Robinson did.

Can't understand how if she wants us so bad, she's makin' us come to her instead of the other way around. And why's she makin' us take the bus to get there?

Doesn't make any sense.

"We gotta move on this, guys."

That's Mel, when he hears Sylvia's offer. "We gotta move on this or we're gonna blow our chance."

That's yesterday. We're having an emergency group meeting, after getting back from New Jersey.

As always, it's me versus Mel.

"This money she's offering us is bullshit, fellas," I say. "We can make that in a couple nights. And the way she's pushing us to sign, I dunno. I say we wait."

"This ain't about a party, nigga!" Mel shoots back. "This lady made the biggest record of all time and she wants to sign us! How the fuck do we say no to her?"

She wants to sign us for not a lot of dough and a whole lotta promises—bookings, tours, publicity, wardrobes, cash, cars, fame and fortune. But there's a whole lot of words on the contract she gave me, and I don't understand any of 'em.

Nobody does.

"Get you a lawyer."

That's what Penny says when I tell her about it.

Where the hell am I gonna get a lawyer?

I talk to Rahiem and he says the same thing. Says his mom and his sister don't want him to sign anything without showing it to a lawyer first.

But he doesn't know any lawyers either.

I run into Big Bank Hank at Disco Fever.

Hank's one of the rappers in the Sugar Hill Gang.

Hank's the man right about now.

Hank's got a whole posse of security guards and five or six fine girls with him. Hank just asked me my name in front of all these people, even though he knows me. Even though everybody in the Bronx knows who I am.

Hank's fronting like he's big shit, but everybody on the street knows he stole his rhymes.

Hank ain't the real.

But Hank's rocking a fur coat, gold chains, and a big limo out front.

Whatever he is, Hank's got it going on.

"Good thing I wasn't there …"

That was Grandmaster Caz of the Cold Crush Brothers, the guy whose rhymes Hank bit. "I woulda kicked his ass all over the club."

We were chillin' at the Hilltop, a private club. It's the kind of off-the-books joint where the windows are blacked out and the door's always locked. The kind of joint where you can get anything you want to stay high until the cows come home: booze, weed, coke, girls, cards, or whatever. But something tells me they don't have anything for my man Caz's troubles.

By now, Caz knows he's been played. Guys have been coming up to him for five months, asking whether that's him on the radio, asking whether he's getting money.

Truth is, right before "Rapper's Delight" came out, Hank was working the door at a club and slinging pizzas out in New Jersey to make the rent.

One day, he goes to Caz and asks to borrow his book of rhymes. Caz gives it to him.

"Next thing I know," Caz says, "Hank's on the radio with some shit I wrote. That bastard bit my rhymes."

Hank's getting paid and Caz isn't.

FLASH'S UNIVERSAL DJ RULE NUMBER FOUR:
Gotta get paid before you get played.

Gotta get my due before somebody bites it from me.
Gotta call the Good Queen.

Now!

ANOTHER ONE BITES THE DUST

There's an old guy on the TV.

His name's Ronald Reagan.

People are saying he's gonna be the next president.

Reagan's asking everybody if we're better off now than we were four years ago.

Am I better off than I was four years ago?

That's a hard one.

Life was easier four years ago, that's for sure. I was just having fun hunting for sound system stuff, buying records, and keeping the beat. Life wasn't any farther from home than Mott Haven Park.

But today, Ronald Reagan's smiling at me, smiling at me from the TV.

The TV's in the backseat of a limo.

The limo is rolling across the George Washington Bridge, on the way to New Jersey, and I'm trying to make up my mind about this Sugar Hill business.

Never been in a limo before.

It's so quiet, I can't hear the motor. Leather smells so nice, I think it might be makin' me high. Damn, I'm watching TV in the backseat of a car!

They show another clip of this Reagan cat. Looks like a movie star.

He smiles just like the Good Queen smiles.

"Beats the bus, huh?" That's Joey Robinson, Sylvia's son. Him and me and the guys—we're all riding in the back of this big, black car, on the way to Sylvia's crib for a signing party. He's joking and smiling, having a good time.

She's the Queen. He's the Prince.

We all roll up to the Sugar Hill offices to sign our recording contracts. It doesn't even take five minutes; we're out of the car, have the papers signed without reading a word, and we're rolling again.

Still doesn't feel right, but I don't have time to think about it.

"Got a surprise for you fellas," Joey says.

Joey throws a tape in the Blaupunkt and cranks it up.

It's the *band* Queen. That hot new jam, "Another One Bites the Dust."

DA-da-Dum. Dum. Dum. Da-da-da-da-DA-da-DUM!

Damn, that's a killer break.

Stereo sounds so good, I don't want to get out of the car . . . until I see the surprise Joey was talking about—the Sugar Hill mansion.

It's a castle . . .

It's a *kingdom* . . .

It's on a piece of land as big as the Greer School!

Whoooa . . . now I definitely feel like I'm on TV.

This joint is lit up like the top of the Empire State Building. The grass is green, the hedges are trimmed, and the flowers all look perfect. The long driveway's full-up with more nice cars.

Just like at the studio, this joint is bigger, cleaner, and newer than anything I've ever seen.

Everybody's speechless. Everybody's thinking the same exact thing: *We need to get some of this.*

Sylvia's waiting for us at the door. Hugs everybody. She doesn't even wait for introductions.

Inside, the crib is packed and the jam's jumping off—disco lights, dance floors, mirror balls, smoke machines. Silk suits and designer dresses, big hair and lots of makeup. One loud-as-hell stereo system.

Everybody's looking good.

Everybody's getting down.

Everybody's loose.

Everybody's having a great time.

I'm excited, but this isn't my spot.

I'm a long way from Disco Fever.

I'm a long way from the Bronx.

I'm a long way from home.

And I'm not dressed for this.

I check out the backyard and people aren't dressed at all. There's a hundred folks out here skinny-dipping in the pool, running around, this and that falling out of bikinis and Speedos. I don't recognize anybody and nobody recognizes me.

I go back inside, hook up with some of the fellas. Sylvia and Joe introduce us around. Try to make everybody feel at ease.

Everybody they introduce us to knows who we are.

Everybody's nice as pie.

But names and faces get confusing and clog up my mind.

I find out later that almost everyone there was either family or Sugar Hill staff.

This crazy shit is too much to handle.

That Queen jam from the car comes on. Now *it's* running around my brain. I look around the room for a DJ, but it's comin' through the stereo.

DA-da-Dum. Dum. Dum.
Another one bites the dust!
Dum. Dum. Dum.
Another one bites the dust!

I'm in a whole new mess of high times.

But I can't shake the feeling that I'm also on a speeding train and I can't get off.

SPIN'S GETTIN' BIGGER

September 1980.
  It's hot.
Hottest summer of my life.
Temperature's rising and so are we.
Grandmaster Flash and the Furious Five MCs got a real record out.

SUGAR HILL RECORDS
"Freedom"
(Tyrone Williams/Ray Smith/Sylvia Robinson/Melvin Glover/Nathaniel Glover/
Keith Wiggins/Guy Williams/Eddie Morris)
GRANDMASTER FLASH
and the FURIOUS FIVE

One day, I step through the door at Richie T's Rhythm Den, a record store over on Tremont Ave. Richie T's got the stereo going. Soon as I'm through the door, I hear kazoos . . . and they sound familiar . . .

Naaaaa-na-na-na-nuh-nuh-nah . . .
Nah-nah-nah-na-nuh-na-na . . .

I ask Richie: "You got my record on the box?"
"Nah, man," he tells me, "that shit there's on the radio!"

Grandmaster Flash and the Furious Five's real record is on the radio!

It's our jam "Freedom." The guys are rapping about their zodiac signs. Mel's a Taurus, Rahiem's an Aquarius, Creole's a Pisces, and Ness, who's a Scorpio, is now known as Scorpio, or Scorp for short. I listen to the rest of the song and watch three people buy our record. Then I call everybody I know and tell 'em the news.

Three weeks later, "Freedom" is rising up the R&B charts and selling out every record store I know.

People love us like they love the Sugar Hill Gang, and the Good Queen is making our dreams come true. "Remember when I told you I knew how to take care of my most valuable assets?" she says after we finish recording the first record. "Well, I've got a surprise."

She shows us outside, where there are six brand-new cars for all of us. Mine is a canary yellow Lincoln Continental.

It's good, 'cause we need the wheels now. We need 'em to keep the appointments we got. We get five calls a day—somebody at the Sugar Hill office telling us what to do, where to go, when we gotta be there.

"Flash, you and the guys need to be up in Harlem for a photo shoot!"

"Flash, you and the guys got a show at the Police Athletic League in Hollis!"

"Flash, get downtown to WBLS . . . Frankie Crocker wants to interview you guys!" Yessir, we're going to WBLS to get on the air with Mister Hollywood himself, the man who's bringing our style to FM radio.

Hollywood.

Chief Rocker.

Frankie Crocker.

This guy is a legend on the air and at every hotspot from Studio 54 all the way to the Apollo. When he walks down the hall of WBLS, people get out of the way like he's royalty. When Hollywood purrs on the microphone, he's smooth as melted butter and cool as an evening breeze.

"That was a new jam to get you high with Grandmaster Flash and the Furious Five . . . 'Freedom.' You heard it first because they brought it *down* to me first, ladies and gentlemen . . . ladies especially, right, Flash?"

I can dig it. I'm getting high in the green room before the show and laid in the limo on the way back home.

———

I'm still spinning at Disco Fever, but my pay goes up. The other nights of the week, the Good Queen's got us on the move, playing shows in Queens, Brooklyn, Staten Island, Long Island, and Newark. Sometimes playing two, three shows a night. Taking care of all the details. All we gotta do is show up.

The spin's getting bigger. And they got people at Sugar Hill to organize everything.

Everything except getting paid. I ask Sylvia one day about how that works and she smiles. "If you ever need money, just come out and see me."

One Friday, "Freedom" breaks the Top 20 on the R&B charts. Time to get paid. I drive out to New Jersey broke, and damn if I don't drive home with three thousand dollars.

First things first.

I put a G on enough blow to get me through the weekend. Then I cop two color TVs—Sony Trinitron—one for Mike and one for me. I also cop me a Betamax. And a water bed.

Then I go over to Paulette Dawson's place with a bunch of groceries for her and the kids. By now, our third, Lalonnie, has been born to the world and she's a little angel.

Paulette's happy to get the goods, but she still hates me for fuckin' her over. Hates me for fuckin' every girl she knows. Can't set foot in that house for more than two minutes without getting into an argument.

She hates me big time when I tell her I'm taking our two oldest, Tawanna and JoJo, out to the park, but actually sneak 'em over to FAO Schwarz and come back with a carload full of toys.

She's trying to teach them values.

I'm trying to buy their love.

And I'm spoiling them rotten.

Then I go over to Jean's house and do the same thing. I look at my other new baby, Kareem, and I can't believe how much he looks just like me. I stare into his shining eyes and I think about what the future holds.

For him.

For me.

For all my kids.

It's peaceful over at Jean's place. Jean's place is a harbor in the storm. Jean's easier to talk to than Paulette One and a lot easier to talk to than Paulette Two.

With Paulette Two, things are complicated. I love her more than life itself, and I know she loves me too.

But we still fight like cats and dogs.

HER: "Who'd my girl Bonnie see you with at Disco Fever last week? Said she saw you getting high with a trifling, skeezey ho she never saw before! Nigga, what'd I tell you about fucking bitches in places where people know who the fuck I am?!"

ME: "Did Bonnie say there were other guys in the club?"

HER: "I don't give a—"

ME: "Did. She. Say. There. Were. Other. Guys. In. The. Club?!"

HER: "NO!"

ME: "Well then how the fuck did she know I was with someone?! How the fuck did she know I wasn't just minding my damn business, trying to have some fun?!"

And it's like that every week. Sure, I'm lying to her face about the girls, and getting high as my kites did back in the day, but telling the truth would only be worse.

The girls aren't the only ones I can't get rid of. Ray Chandler's around too. Mad as he is, thinking he should have gotten a cut of the records with Bobby and Sylvia, he's still doing his thing, still promoting shows, still making that money.

One day toward the end of the year, he calls me up with a proposal:

"I got the Hotel Diplomat for Christmas Eve. I also got the Funky Four, the Fantastic Freaks, and Kurtis Blow. But I need y'all, and I need y'all to help me promote it. Make an appearance out at all them high schools in Queens."

I know the Hotel Diplomat is no joke. It's even bigger than the Audubon, and between the hype and the bill, Ray tells me he's charging twenty bucks a head to get in.

I do the math.

That's eighty thousand bucks.

I tell him what I want for the set and it's a big number. He tells me no. He makes a scene and tells me he's gotta pay Kurtis and his manager. Then he tells me he's got another twenty-five thousand on top of that to rent the joint. He goes on and on about this bill and that bill, but when I tell him I'm about to walk, he agrees . . .

So long as I can get the Furious Five to do the promos.

I talk to the guys. They agree to play the show but everybody's too busy to help sell tickets. Ray gets pissed. "Then you tell 'em they ain't getting one penny more than what they always get."

I know what that means. Means trouble.

The night of the jam, the place is packed. Mel and the guys show up, take one look at the crowd, and say they want a thousand bucks each.

"We're the reason these walls sweating, yo," says Mel. Ray might have had him beat three years ago, but he doesn't have shit on him these days, and Mel knows it.

Ray starts to bust a blood vessel, but holds it back. "Y'all didn't promote this show, I did."

"We're top-billing," says Rahiem, "and you're paying us sardine money."

Ray looks at Rahiem and I can see a fight coming.

"Just how much you think you're worth, boy?" Ray growls.

The guys walk.

This is bad.

How do I spin my way out of this?

THE BAD QUEEN

September 1981.

 11:24 A.M.

The clock radio's blaring my jam . . .

And by that, I mean *my jam*. "The Adventures of Grandmaster Flash on the Wheels of Steel."

It's the newest record I've got. It's also the first record ever that's a pure DJ solo. No house band. No rappers. No Sylvia Robinson telling me what to do . . . just me, my gear, my beats, and my techniques.

After months of asking, the Good Queen finally let me do my thing. After months of standing around the studio, letting live musicians play what I could be mixing on two turntables, and showing the engineers how to mix everybody's voice so the record sounds right, I finally got my own record. Finally got to punch-phase, cut, cue, spin back, rub, and zuka-zuka on wax. Kept coming back and coming back on the Good Queen:

"Gimme a shot. No rappers on this one, Sylvia. This one's my show. People are gonna listen, trust me." Finally, she says yes.

Except we're out on tour.

So the Good Queen flies me and Mel home for a day to record it. Flies us home.

Doesn't even take that long, though. I take all my favorite jams, throw 'em in the pot, mix 'em up, record the whole thing live in three takes, and a week later, we drop it on the people.

SUGAR HILL RECORDS

"The Adventures of Grandmaster Flash on the Wheels of Steel"

(Jiggs Chase/Melvin Glover/George Jackson/Sylvia Robinson)

GRANDMASTER FLASH

Might be my name on the record and my name on the group, but it's still *our* jam. What's good for me is good for the guys—and vice versa—at least that's the way I see it.

It's not the way Mel sees it, though.

It's not the way Sylvia sees it either. Especially now that she's got the Funky Four Plus One, the West Street Mob, Sequence, Spoonie Gee and Kool Moe Dee and Treacherous Three on the label. "I really want to get you guys back in the studio," she said, smiling to our faces, last time we were out there, "but I got my hands full with other projects at the moment."

I'm thinking: That's bullshit, lady. We could write rhymes and cut records all day long if you'd let us, and they'd still sell out in a minute ...

But I don't say that to her face.

Maybe I should. Maybe I should tell her we're not happy. Maybe I should tell her my group, Grandmaster Flash and the Furious Five, is the hottest act she's got and she needs to remember it.

Maybe I need to tell all that to her face, at the meeting we got this morning ...

The clock radio snaps me back: "...That was Grandmaster Flash, taking you for an adventure on the Wheels of Steel ... at eleven-twenty-eight in the A.M. on WBLS."

...the meeting we got in exactly thirty-two minutes from now!

Oh shit!

Did I really get that wild last night?

I sit up in bed ... the one I share with Paulette Jeffrey. I look around ... two girls—neither one of 'em named Paulette—three empty Moët bottles and four lines of coke on the nightstand.

Yeah ... I got that wild last night.

I do one of the lines, freeze another, and leave the other two for the ladies, for when they wake up.

I don't remember who's who, but if they're still here and Paulette gets home, it's gonna be bad.

I throw on my clothes, stumble down four flights of stairs and out into the way-too-bright sunshine.

Into the way-too-real world.

"Oh damn! You're Grandmaster Flash!" There's a young b-boy on the curb, staring up at me with eyes so big, it hurts me just to squint at 'em. "I snuck into Danceteria last month, that night you were there . . . You were rockin' it harder than I ever seen anybody rock a show before!"

Gotta find my car . . .

"You seen a canary yellow Lincoln Continental around here somewhere?"

The kid shakes his head.

Where's my damn car?

Two hours later, I finally get to New Jersey. Had to call a cab and borrow sixty-eight bucks from the Queen to pay the fare 'cause I'm broke. My mouth is dry, my stomach empty, my eyes buggin' out, and my head about to explode.

And I still don't even know where my car is.

When I get in the conference room, the Good Queen's smiling. She's telling me she's happy to see me. The Good Queen's also telling me that my jam didn't do as well as everyone thought it would.

I don't get it . . . if the song isn't doing so great, then why's it been all over the radio for the past three months?

"Welllll," she hedges, "what they play on the radio and what they sell in the stores isn't always the same thing. Rap still isn't catching on the way we'd hoped it would. Of course, *we* still believe in you, but we need to pace things a little. Come up with a strategy. I know you understand that this is how the business works, Flash."

Except I don't understand.

The way business works is we're selling out every show Joe Senior books for us. By now, she's got us on the road to Boston, Philly, and Pittsburgh. Mel just got a whole new wardrobe. I'm hearing more and more of the old kids from the Bronx on the radio. If we're not selling records, how come everybody knows who we are? If business is so slow, how come we're getting interviewed on TV?

Besides, I got friends around the Sugar Hill office, and they tell me different stories than Sylvia does. They tell me the Good Queen's not all smiles when we're not around. They tell me she gets pissed off. They say she storms around saying the Furious Five—and Grandmaster Flash in particular—are getting uppity. Says she's gonna put us down for a while and put up the other acts, like Sequence.

Maybe the Good Queen ain't so good after all ...

As for the meeting today, it's no use. I keep trying to say how we have some heat right about now, thanks to all the work we've been putting in. We got the lyrics to a new song and I'm looking for a hook. Time's right to get another record out, and fast.

But the Bad Queen ain't having it, and the meeting ends with me on one end of an argument and Sylvia on another. Mel tries to make things right between us but it's no use. And like it or not, we're not going into the studio anytime soon.

I hitch a ride back to E-Z Mike's place with Rahiem. When I get home, I make a few calls about my car. The cops don't know anything and neither do my people on the street ... so it can't be stolen.

I call the impound yard ... I don't *think* I got towed last night, but then again you never know ... but they ain't got it either.

Where the hell is my car?

On a hunch, I call the leasing company.

They tell me Sugar Hill Records closed out the lease.

The car's been repossessed.

The message is clear:

Don't fuck with the Queen.

We lay low for a few months. Play shows outta town, hit up black radio whenever we can, rock the Fever every Tuesday night. It's time to party a little, mend fences a little ... take it easy a little.

Time to live life, smell the roses, and keep the beat.

We rock a few gigs in Boston and I see a lovely lady in the crowd, every show. There's something about her—something magical—which I can sense when she dances; this lady locks the beat down with the nod of her head but moves her body to a secret inner rhythm. Every player in the house steps up to her, but she easily, gently brushes them off.

After the show, *I* step up to her. "I'm the one they call Flash," I say, smooth as I can. Usually that's all it takes and I'm in.

But this woman's different.

"I know," she laughs. "I'm Joanne. I love what you and the guys do." Something in this woman's voice tells me she's impervious to false charm. She's not mean or aggressive, but she's not taking the bait.

One thing's clear about Joanne (not her real name) right from jump street: she's not like other women.

Joanne's sexy, smart, and always down with a smile and a good attitude. She says she loves the band, but doesn't want anything in return for her compliment.

Eventually, we get to know each other. Joanne even hips me to healthy eating. She teaches me about the benefits of juices and macrobiotic food. We talk about vitamins and minerals. Joanne's clean as a whistle. When I'm around her, I don't get high.

Joanne's a breath of fresh air right when I need it. She's got something I want . . . and I'm not just talking about booty. There's something inside this woman—an inner light that creates peace in her life as well as mine when I'm around her.

It even washes over into my relationships with the guys and with the folks at Sugar Hill.

I find an import record on Island by the Tom Tom Club called "Genius of Love" and it gives me an idea for the next single. I share it with Mel and he agrees, we get back in the groove and put the new record out easier than we've ever put one out. Even the Queen is pleased.

To top it off, this cat named Charlie Ahearn makes a movie called *Wild Style*. It's not just a movie about hip hop, it's about the life I'm living. It shows a big battle between the Fantastic Freaks and the Cold Crush Brothers and Double Trouble freestyling a flow; it shows graffiti kids and b-boys getting down; it even shows rich people from downtown getting hip to what's happening uptown. And thanks to my man FAB 5 FREDDY introducing me to Charlie and Blondie, who was huge at the time, *Wild Style* shows me doing my thing on the turntables in the kitchen of Jean's house.

Wild Style puts me in the movies.

For a rare moment, it's smooth sailing.

———

December 1981.

I haven't seen my mom in a good while. Penny and Lilly have been on my ass to go.

They say Mom's not doing so hot; that she's not well in her mind again.

Everybody's saying Mom's getting worse.

Everybody's saying, "Better go see her soon."

So I do. And I bring some groceries with me.

"You look thin, Butsy," she says. "Let me make you something to eat."

As she's cooking, she throws on an Ella Fitzgerald LP.

A blast from the past. It's magic medicine for Mommy.

The strings rise and I watch the muscles in her face ease up. Mom smiles all the way up to her eyes. Mom still loves Ella. Mom still loves me too. Still calls me her baby boy while we're sitting together at the kitchen table.

Mom takes my hand in hers. Even after all those years at the sewing machine, her hand is soft, warm, and dry to the touch. It's fragile, and I'm worried I might hold it too hard, but I don't let go. And when she squeezes my hand, I can feel a little magic medicine of my own.

Mom is still Mom.

For a moment or two before Christmas of 1981, everything's cool. Still, I can't help but think ...

Is the music ever gonna be safe like it used to be?

THE MESSAGE

May 1982.

We got a new jam.

It's big.

It's *really* big.

It's *fucking huge.*

But every time I hear it, I get the same sinking feeling in my gut . . .

I'm losing something here.

Been feeling this feeling for months now. Got me creeping around the Sugar Hill office on the low. Got me laid up at night, unable to sleep. Got me doing more coke than ever, just to maintain. But even with the coke, I can't get this feeling outta my head.

It's like a jungle sometimes, it makes me wonder
How I keep from going under

That's the song.

That's the message.

That's the song, "The Message."

And that's exactly what I'm thinking and feeling when I hear it for the first time. The Queen's been on the group to record "The Message" for almost a year. One day she came to us with a fragment of something Ed Fletcher—the percussionist in the house band—had written.

"It's gonna be huge," she kept saying. "It's gonna be the biggest song we've ever done. Bigger than 'Rapper's Delight.'"

But nobody in the group liked it. Not at first, anyway—the shit was way too dark, way too edgy, and way too much of a downer. It was the furthest thing from a party rap anyone could imagine. The first verse alone was talking about broken glass, pissing in the streets, being homeless, having your car towed, and getting jacked by baseheads.

Don't push me 'cause I'm close to the edge

Slowly and surely, the Queen stayed on our asses to do "The Message."
HER: "Have you guys been listening to that cassette?"
ME: "Uh, a little bit."
HER (a couple months later): "What do you think about it?"
ME (a couple months later): "Ehh . . . it's alright."
HER (a couple months after that): "It's a real good idea . . ."
HER (a couple more months after that): "You hear the new music?"
ME: "This isn't what we do," I think to myself.
HER: "You guys are the ones to do this song. Do it however you think is right, but *do it*."

Sylvia keeps pushing us to do the song every chance she gets.

Every time, I pray she drops the whole thing.

Then something starts to happen.

I'm at Paulette Jeffrey's place the first time.

It's the first time since I-don't-know-when that we've spent the whole day together. Just the two of us. No drugs on me, no yelling on her, the Delfonics' "For the Love I Gave to You" is playing in the background. The sun goes down and we get up to go into the city to see *E.T.* when the phone rings.

"Mel's out at the mansion," a friend of mine from the office tells me when I pick up. "Where the hell are you?"

What the hell's going on? And why am I getting cut out of the loop? I call Mel. He lies to me when I ask about the meeting.

"You know how it is, Flash," he says. "Me and the wife and the baby were just chillin'. Nothing to get all paranoid about."

But that's just what happens, and it only gets worse when it happens three more times.

Eventually we're in the studio, doing this record nobody believes in. We bring form to the fragment of Ed Fletcher's idea. Only the Queen believes in it . . . and what the Queen wants, the Queen gets. The record isn't all she wants now, either.

HER: "We want Mel to do the song by himself this time around."

This is what I was afraid of. This is how things fall apart. This isn't about Grandmaster Flash and the Furious Five. This isn't everybody shining at the same time. This isn't about teamwork. This isn't about taking five MCs and making 'em sound like one, which has been our thing from the very beginning.

This is about Mel.

This is about Sylvia.

This is about money.

It's also about Ed Fletcher—a.k.a. "Duke Bootee"—rapping instead of the rest of the guys. How the hell did he get in the mix?

I make one final plea to make this song about the group—all five guys—and not just Mel, and the Queen shuts me down, flat.

HER: "Mel's doing the rap. That's how this one's going to be."

So that's what all those meetings were about?

I take Sylvia aside and I beg her: "Please don't do this. Don't do this to my group. Don't make this record about one MC when it took me almost ten years to perfect what we—"

"Flash," she interrupts, "a hit is a hit." The Queen smiles and that's the end of the discussion.

Don't push me 'cause I'm close to the edge

I'm trying not to lose *my* head, and I'm also trying not to lose my group . . .

But I think I'm losing both.

In the end, the only thing we get on "The Message" is our name. I hate the fact that it's on the song—a song we had nothing to do with. The only thing I recognize from the old days is a few lyrics Mel chops up and scrambles into his last verse.

What I hear between the lines is all the pent-up anger Mel's got.

I hear how he feels like he's got to get over before he goes under.

I hear how he sees the world as a hostile place.

I can't help but wonder whether he sees me as a threat too.

"The Message" isn't a song about the place I came from or the people I grew up with. This isn't anything I helped to create. I listen to the tracks over and over again and I can't understand how it's come to this.

When the final mix is done, Sylvia jumps for joy—the song came in at seven minutes and eleven seconds.

Seven-eleven. The Queen's lucky numbers.

"This is gonna be great," she squeals. "This record is going to be huge! I can feel it!"

SUGAR HILL RECORDS

"The Message"

(Edward Fletcher/Melvin Glover/Sylvia Robinson/Jiggs Chase)

GRANDMASTER FLASH

and the FURIOUS FIVE

A week later, the Queen sends me and Cowboy to Frankie Crocker with an advance copy; tells us to go make ourselves useful. We hit the dope spot on the way and get blown out of our minds. When we get to the radio station, Frankie debuts the record, and high as I am, I can feel the energy in the DJ booth jump up when Frankie plays Sugar Hill single number SH-584-A.

The Queen was right on the money.

"The Message" is a hit.

The next day, every radio station in New York gets a copy. If I switch on the radio, I can turn the dial from WBLS to WKTU to WKRS and hear "The Message" playing on all of 'em, all at the same time . . .

Or in succession . . .

Or twice in a row.

"The Message" blows up.

"The Message" puts us on a whole other level of the game. The word's getting back that we're blowing up the radio in Los Angeles, Chicago, Seattle, Atlanta, Dallas, Miami, and every other urban market in the country. Even still, I can't shake this feeling.

I'm losing something here.

I've always known what to do, where to go, and how to get by. I've always been the guy calling the shots and keeping the beat. But once again, I find myself asking the same old question . . .

What happens now?

"GOTTA GET MY ASS A LAWYER"

A month after we release "The Message," *Billboard* reports that we've gone gold. But I'm still broke. I scrape by on gigs, but between everything I got going with kids and women and the dope man, the money never lasts.

Me and Cowboy roll out to New Jersey to get some money from the Queen one Monday after I read the figures in *Billboard*. Gotta get paid for all this hard work we've been doing. Soon as I walk through the door, I notice new platinum records hanging on the walls, not gold ones. The labels say, "The Message."

"When did this happen?" I ask the receptionist.

"Last Tuesday," she says. "We just got word from the distributor they shipped two million copies."

Two.

Million.

Records.

Holy shit.

How come nobody told us?

"They look like they been spray-painted," I say.

"Sylvia had 'em done up over the weekend," she says.

This doesn't make any sense. The magazine said we've sold five hundred thousand singles. But we've shipped two million. There's fake plati-num records on the wall. And on top of it all, me and Cowboy don't have money for the rent. I look at him and he looks at me . . .

Who we s'posed to believe here?

In the other room, I hear Joe shouting in the phone: "I don't need anyone to tell me I have a double-platinum record . . . I just need to count the money!"

How come we're not counting the money?

"I gotta be honest with you, Flash," Sylvia says when I ask her about all this. "We're not doing so hot out there. Sequence is doing bad, Funky Four is doing really bad, and Treacherous Three? We can't *give* those records away."

"What about us?" I say. Whether we're gold, platinum, or double plati-num, I *know* we're hot.

"Welllll . . . it's not that people don't like the record," she says, "but all that time you spent in the studio cost us a lot of money."

Waitaminute . . . she told us to get in there and make the song work however we could, and now she's saying all this is OUR fault?!

She goes on. "Plus there's the new outfits you guys ordered . . . travel expenses . . . publicity and promotions . . . not to mention more than a few busted-up hotel rooms. And let's not forget that time I bailed every-body out for the helicopter incident." Gotta give her that one; not that long ago, our road manager hopped the tour bus without paying for a prostitute the night before. She got pissed off, called the cops, and they put a helicopter on our asses.

The Queen goes on and on, but finally drops a lead weight on my foot: "I can check with accounting, but you guys probably have the label in the hole for something in the neighborhood of four hundred thousand dollars, give or take a few."

This ain't right.

Hookers and tore-up hotel rooms or no, we've done six records with this lady. While the Sugar Hill Gang's been falling off, we've stayed on top. Me and the fellas are the ones keeping her on the throne. Now she's tell-ing us that we're costing her all this money, like she's been doing *us* the favor all along?

This.

Ain't.

Right.

A week later, the Queen calls: "I know you've been worried about money, and I've got some good news. You and the guys are going out on tour. It's a big one too, the biggest yet."

We got stops in all the cities where the record's been hot. Not only that, we're headlining the tour. Headlining over acts like the Commodores and the Bar-Kays. All because of this one song.

We hit the road and deliver "The Message." Three weeks worth of shows and the money I'm making should have me feeling fine, but it doesn't.

Can't stop thinking about all those records.

Can't stop thinking about some papers I saw around the office. Papers calling me a non-affiliate, saying everyone but Mel is "N/A." Don't know what N/A means but I get that sinking feeling in my gut just the same. Can't help thinking that it has something to do with business and money. Gotta admit that even if I wasn't high all the time, I don't know much about handling my business *or* my money.

Can't stop thinking about the names on the labels of the records themselves. Mel's name is on 'em. So's Jiggs's, our producer. So's Sylvia's, even though she didn't write any of our stuff.

Where are the names of the rest of the fellas? And how come Mel's been bullying everybody to write the rhymes himself, when the rest of the guys used to write all their own rhymes?

I get my answer one of the nights out on the road. We're laid up in Washington, D.C., and Scorp's throwing the after-party. By the time I get there, it's jumping off.

Soon as I walk through the door, a tall brother with a lanky strut grabs me by the arm. He's all gold and leather and spandex.

He's Rick James.

We've been sharing top billing with him for the past few nights and this nigga rocks the house harder than anybody I've ever seen. He's got a quick wit and a quicker tongue and he's also one of the nicest guys I've ever met.

Twenty minutes later, everybody's loose and Rick's talking fast: "I love what y'all are doin' to rap. Been meaning to tell you that. Shit man, you ain't doin' it to it, you practically invented it. Shiiiiiit . . . you're shining a big bright light on some kinda new black poetry."

When this cat talks, I listen. I've been playing his records for years and I love every one of 'em. Now he's saying he's digging us. Forget about all the drama I got in my life; for a moment, I'm grooving that Rick James is a fan of mine.

"Listen up," he says, "I wanna do a record with you. You got a deal rider from the label for that?"

"Deal rider?" I ask him. "What you talking about?"

There's that feeling again . . .

"Your publishing deal, man!" he says, like he's talking about going to the barbershop. "I gotta buy you out, or does the label own a piece of this shit if we put it together?"

ME: "What's publishing?"

Rick's jaw hits the floor. Suddenly, the sinking feeling's washing over me stronger than the drugs I'm on. Suddenly, I don't even feel high anymore.

Rick spends the next hour explaining publishing, writing credits, mechanical royalties, performance royalties, and everything else I don't know about the business of music. I got a feeling those papers I signed three years ago don't speak to any of it.

"You mean to tell me nobody ever talked to you about this shit?" he asks.

I shake my head.

Rick whistles long and low.

The next day we hop the tour bus and head back home. All the way, I can't stop thinking about all the shit Rick was saying. I wanna confront Sylvia about this, but I'm afraid of her. Don't know what she's gonna say. Don't know what she's gonna do.

But I gotta do something.

That evening, we pull into the lot back at the office. I just wanna go home, but there's talk about doing Joey Robinson's eighteenth birthday party out at the mansion tonight. I'm tired and I just want to go home.

Just when I think it can't get any worse, Joey pulls into the lot and I can't believe what I see . . .

Joey's behind the wheel of a brand-new red Corvette with a giant white bow wrapped all the way around the whole car. He pulls in front of the bus and jumps out of the car, lookin' over at his mom like he just lucked up and won the lottery.

If the label's doing so bad, how come this kid just got a car with a bow on it?

I think back to all the things Rick told me and the next thing that comes to my mind is six words:

Gotta get my ass a lawyer.

"PACK YOUR BAGS, FLASH . . ."

Y ou're going to Europe."

That's the latest word from Sylvia. It's also the most words she has said to me since we got back into town that night.

Since I asked her one little question . . .

"What's publishing?"

That was in November of last year. When I asked it, the color ran out of her face, even if that old smile stayed put. And just like that, I was outta the loop. Stopped getting invited to group meetings completely.

I ask the guys about Sylvia and they say, "I don't know, Flash, she's pretty upset with you." They make her sound nice, but I know the salt she's throwing when I'm not around.

"Flash is just the DJ."

"He's not one of the lyricists."

"We don't need his ass anymore."

I know because my friends at the office tell me so. I also know Sylvia's saying other things too.

"Flash is asking questions."

"Flash wants to see accounting statements."

"Fuckin' Flash got himself a goddamn lawyer."

I took Rick James's advice. Found a guy I could do business with named Morton Berger who, in trade for managing the band, took on the case. Started calling the Queen, writing letters, and filing papers.

Now it's March 1983, and I'm getting the silent treatment.

I hear the guys are working on a new single, "New York, New York." It's the third one since "The Message" hit, but the first time I hear any of 'em is on the radio.

These days, I got a whole new monkey on my back, and the little guy is chattering in my ear about everything I can't handle right at this minute. What's worse, no matter how much coke I sniff, I can't shake the feeling of being alone. Can't shake the feeling I'm not in control anymore. Can't shake the hate in my heart. Can't be there for my kids, can't hardly keep the beat.

When it comes to getting paid, I *can* keep my head above water, but only thanks to Terrible Tuesdays, and I'm hardly loving it anymore. Ain't looking for new jams or sharpening my skills; just spinning the same old records and cutting the same old bullshit I did last Tuesday ... and the Tuesday before that. Waiting for somebody to pass me a gram or two to play a request. Counting the minutes before I can pack up my gear, get out, and get high.

Tonight, the monkey's messing with me bad. I catch a cab up into Harlem up to Skee-Ball's crib. Skee-Ball's a dealer I know who's always holding and always generous.

I sit down.

I break out with the shit.

Start chopping.

Bend down ...

Put the straw up my nose and ...

SNNNNFFFFF!!

Nothing.

Again ...

SNNNNFFFFF!!

I don't even feel it hit.

Suddenly, I feel a falling sensation—like I'm gonna fall right through the chair I'm sitting in. For a second, I think it might be the high after all, but all the bad thoughts are still polluting my mind. Thoughts of the band, of Sylvia, thoughts of my family, all of it. Can't shake the thoughts of everything in my life that's gone so wrong. Can't shake this monkey on my back, trying to pull me down.

This has gotta be my worst nightmare, come to life.

Worse than losing the band.

Worse than getting ripped off.

Worse than losing everything I got.

Can't get high.

So I start to shake.

Then I start to yell.

Then my nose starts to bleed.

What the fuck am I gonna do now?!

Skee-Ball comes to the rescue. I must be screaming my head off by now, 'cause he grabs me by the shoulders ...

Pulls out a glass water pipe ...

Puts it in front of me ...

Takes out a little white pebble ...

Puts it on the screen ...

Holds a lighter over the rock ...

And he simply says one word:

"Suck."

KA-THOOOMM!!!

Hits like a soft bomb inside my chest and blooms like a beautiful flower. Makes every cell in my body vibrate and hum. Doesn't stop until it comes out through the nails on my fingers and the hairs on my head.

Shiiiiiiiit, I even feel happy in my eyelashes.

I am back on.

I am high again.

I did not know a human being could feel this good.

AAHHHHHHHHHHHHHHHHHHHHHHHHHH ...

I'm high on a heavyweight punch and the monkey's long gone. I forget about all the badness I gotta deal with and I drift away on a cloud. Feels like I'm fallin' in love for the first time and I don't care if I ever come back.

But the next morning, the Queen calls.

"Pack your bags, Flash. You're going to Europe."

Turns out "The Message" is blowing up over in England and Germany and there's money to be made. Banned from the office or not, the promoters still ask for me by name and the Queen's no dummy.

They tell me Europe is nice.

They tell me the old buildings are beautiful, that the girls love us, the crowds get wild, the fans grab at us the second we get off the bus, and the food is delicious. I wouldn't know. I only leave my hotel room to go to the show or the bus or the plane. I keep my eyes shut when it's daylight. I ain't about to share my dope with no chick. I can't hear anything when we're onstage 'cause I can't wait to get offstage and get high. I smoke coke for breakfast, lunch, and dinner.

I have only one moment of clarity.

We're on the bus, headed through London. Must be the 'hood part of town, 'cause I see something that gets my attention. There's a concrete wall with a gigantic graffiti bomb thrown up—top to bottom, end to end. Thirty feel long and ten feet high. Colorful and energetic and full of life, just like home.

Looking at this piece all the way over here in England, I suddenly get the feeling that what we're doing is much bigger than I thought it was, or ever thought it would be. It's bigger than the band. Bigger than Herc and Bam and Cold Crush and Kurtis and Sugar Hill. Bigger than the graffiti writers or the b-boy crews.

Hip hop.

It's bigger than the Bronx.

Bigger than New York.

Bigger than America.

This music, this scene, this ... *thing* is here to stay. This *thing* I helped create has been born to the world.

Part of me is in awe.

Part of me is in despair.

Part of me is in rage.

Oh well.

I still got plenty of base left.

TRICKLE-DOWN GARBAGE

You're going on *Soul Train.*"

May 1983.

Never dreamed of being on TV, much less on *Soul Train.*

Been watching *Soul Train* since jump street. Watching the performers like they were the funky kings and queens of the universe ... every one of 'em—Michael and his brothers, Smokey and the Godfather, Cheryl Lynn and the Impressions, the Whispers and the Moments and the Intruders and the Four Tops, and *dag* ... who *hasn't* been on that show? Watching and wondering and thinking what it would be like to get a taste.

Now I'm getting a taste. Now I'm getting all I can eat ... if I'm even interested.

My mind's a mess.

I go over to my baby sister Lilly's house a week before we're s'posed to fly out to LA. First time I've seen her since "The Message" hit. When I tell her the news, she starts screaming and yelling: *"My brother's goin' on* Soul Train*! My big brother's gonna be on TV!"*

She doesn't know any better.

She doesn't know that I haven't even talked to the guys since we got back from Europe. She doesn't know that I've been talking to A&R guys from a bunch of different labels, thanks to what Rick James and Morton Berger told me. She doesn't know that my life has nothing to do with music and everything to do with attorneys right about now. She doesn't know that I haven't been in front of a turntable in over a month.

She doesn't know that I'm already trippin' about staying properly high when I'm on *Soul Train*. She doesn't know I gotta smoke in her bathroom 'cause I can't wait until I get home.

What she doesn't know is killing me.

Lilly knows something's up, though, because she gets Penny on the phone while I'm over there. Before I know it, I got my big sister on the line. Actually, she's got me . . .

PENNY: "Butsy, what's up with you?"

ME: "Everything's great. Lilly tell you about *Soul Train*?"

PENNY: "I'm talking about that grimy stuff."

ME: "What stuff?"

PENNY: "Don't even try. I know how you're smoking that base."

ME: "*I* don't fuck with that."

PENNY: "Paulette Jeffrey knows who you cop from, not to mention she's been trying to call you for three weeks. *What the fuck is wrong with you, Butsy?!*"

That explains why nobody's selling me any real weight; even the dealers are scared of Paulette Two. I can always get a free taste, but the second I pull out my wallet, they can't do nothing for me.

Penny keeps on screaming in my ear in one long sentence:

"Damn, Flash, why you gotta make it so hard for people to love you everybody's worried and if Mom and them found out you wouldn't even know the end of it so hear me when I say to you DON'T FUCK WITH THAT SHIT!"

With that, she slams the phone down. My big sis has a mouth and a temper. My big sis likes to party as much as me. But beneath all that, my big sis is scared because she loves me.

Penny's sick of seeing me get messed around, either by the drugs or by the Queen.

"This bitch is ripping you off left and right," Penny shouts when I tell her of a show Sylvia's making us do before we leave for LA to go on *Soul Train*. "That ain't right, Flash. That ain't right at all."

Penny hasn't liked Sylvia from day one and hasn't been afraid to say so.

Hasn't trusted her since she found out about the contract. Hasn't had a kind word to say since the Queen's been getting rich off our jams while we walk around with empty pockets.

"Look at you, Flash! She's got your gold records on her walls and you don't have a decent change of clothes or money to buy a goddamn drink at the Fever!"

I hate to admit it, but Penny's right. Me and the guys are broke as we go play a show for Sylvia at a high-class downtown joint called the Ritz. Fact is, we're so broke we need to ask Penny for a ride to the club.

We show at the Ritz an hour and a half late.

The Queen's Rolls is parked out front.

We unload our gear.

But the bouncer stops us at the door and says, "Sylvia says y'all got to pay the cover to get inside. Ten bucks a head."

It takes me a minute to figure it out:

We're headlining this show.

Sylvia's collecting all the profits for tonight.

She's making us pay to play our own show.

This *definitely* ain't right.

"Serves you right for being late!" Sylvia scolds when she comes outside to see what's going on. "And another thing: if you still wanna play *Soul Train*, you're giving me an apology."

Then she turns to face me. I can tell by the look in her eye that this ain't gonna be fun.

"Especially you, Flash," the Queen says, waving a finger with a huge diamond ring in my face. "I hear anything else about lawsuits or people asking questions about things that's nobody's business, you're through."

Suddenly Penny's in the Queen's face.

"Just who the hell you think you talking to? My little brother mighta grown up learning to respect his momma and get intimidated by a woman, but I ain't scared of you, bitch. You see that diamond on your finger? He bought it for you! And if you think he's gonna keep making it rain the way you been treating him, you got another thing coming!"

It's ugly. Penny's screaming at Sylvia. Sylvia's screaming at Penny. Both of 'em looking like they're gonna chew the other one's face off.

Security steps in. And though she might be my big sister, Penny ain't nobody to them, and Sylvia pays the bills.

As Penny's dragged away, she gets the last word in: "You might take his money, but you ain't gonna take his talent."

The Queen says nothing to Penny. She says nothing to me. But she gives me a look that says it all . . .

. . . Time to go onstage, Flash.

Time to go sing for the privilege of being on my record label.

With that look, the Queen tells me she's taken something more important from me than my money or my talent—she's taken my self-esteem.

Beneath all the bullshit, I still love having my group. I still love this thing we got, even with all the fights. Even if we don't talk anymore. That's what I'm thinking the day we tape the show. Even though we fly out to LA together, we don't talk much anymore. Our thoughts and goals are no longer unified. We meet up and do the "The Message" with all the trimmings. Our thing—especially with this song—is way more than a concert. It's like a Broadway show. This song's got a story, and we act it out on *Soul Train.*

When Mel finishes his first verse, I pretend to sock him in the jaw and he hits the floor. Rahiem raps the King Kong verse while me and Creole pretend to stomp Cowboy's guts out. I can't help but think we didn't used to do shit like this when we did our own songs.

Still, the crowd eats it up like pancakes. People screaming and shouting "East Coast!" like we brought our own audience with us. One way or another, love each other or hate each other, we're kings of this new scene. Somewhere in my heart, I know there's hope.

The feeling doesn't last, though. We finish the jam and Don Cornelius swoops over for the interview. Rahiem does most of the talking and gives me the shine: "He's the baddest thing on two turntables." Meanwhile, Scorpio's prowling around the stage with a baseball bat, like he's about to bust a jack-move. Carrying on like he's still part of the show. I see how that's the deal with us: even when the show stops, the drama continues. And when Don mentions Joey and Sylvia Robinson—how he's close personal friends with the whole Sugar Hill family—it snaps me back to the bullshit at hand.

We're set to do another song, so we chill backstage while Evelyn

"Champagne" King sings "Betcha She Don't Love You." It's now or never, and I tell the guys what's on my mind.

"Sylvia's been playing us. All those records we sell, we haven't seen a dime. And for what? Rented cars? Fish scales? All the pussy we can hit? We could live easy off this song, yet here we are with nickel-and-dime change."

Mel's the first one to speak. "There you go again. '*We* could be living so large off this song . . . This lady's playing *us*.' *We* and *us* ain't got nothing to do with *you* . . . Talking all this trash like *you* had something to do with making these records. *You* didn't! *You* just a DJ! And these days? Shiiiiit . . . all you do is get high and jump around."

For a moment, I see red. I want to remind Mel about the truth. I want to tell him that the DJ gave birth to the MC.

There would be no such thing as the MC without the DJ.

I want to tell him he better not *ever* forget it.

Instead, I set aside the hurt that Mel's words do. I set aside my anger and pain, 'cause the other guys are still listening to what I have to say. "You just heard Don Cornelius say it," I tell the rest of the guys. "We got the biggest rap jam ever. We can live off the tour bookings for the next six months, find another label, and fight for what's ours if we play it right. But we gotta stand up together. I've been talking to a guy over at Elektra records who says he got no problem giving us publishing and royalties, *buying* us some cars and all the stuff we should've had in the—"

"*The hell you say, Flash!*" Mel's screaming now. "Sugar Hill ain't robbin' nobody! If it weren't for them, where would we be?"

For a second I think about all the cats we came up with. Herc's out of the picture and off the map; he got stabbed at one of his own parties a few years ago and he hasn't played since. Even before that, guys like him and Caz and the rest of the Cold Crush Brothers stayed in the Bronx, while we went international.

For better or worse, some guys simply never took it to the next level.

Mel continues to scream at me: "*Are you that high, nigga?!* You think people are gonna remember who the fuck we are if we don't turn out another hit in two months?! Shiiiit, I owe everything I got to Sugar Hill!"

Suddenly, it all makes sense.

Mel's name is on the labels and the papers.

Mel's been hustling to write all the raps by himself.

Mel's got money.

No wonder he's playing the Queen's side.

Mel's got something to lose.

I ask around to the rest of the guys, but they don't wanna rock the boat. Sylvia's been feeding 'em some kind of Reaganomics trickle-down garbage about how if the label doesn't do good, they don't do good, and how if we don't stay hot, the train doesn't leave the station. But what they don't understand is that she's eating cake and we're crumb-snatching.

Fuck Reaganomics.

I tell 'em about Morton Berger and Rick James and what they think we can get. I tell 'em our name is all we need. I tell 'em, "If y'all can write rhymes and bust routines and I continue rockin' these turntables, we can be as bad as we wanna be, so long as we got our name."

There's a long silence.

Then Cowboy finally says, "Mighta been the Flash show back in the day, but times have changed. And if it ain't broke, don't fix it, you know what I mean?"

Silence again. Nobody looks me in the eye.

A stagehand comes in the green room and tells us we're up in sixty seconds.

Discussion's over. We gotta go.

We take the *Soul Train* stage again and run through "The Message II." The whole time, I got a feeling in my chest like nothing I've ever felt before.

It's hard for me to breathe.

MO & JOE

Coming back from LA, reality sets in—the old days are gone.

I might have only been feeling that feeling a couple months ago, but I'm knowing it now—my group isn't mine anymore.

Maybe it's Mel's group.

Maybe it's Sylvia's group.

All I know is I don't call the shots.

Instead, I call Joe Robinson, the behind-the-scenes king of Sugar Hill Records. The feeling in my gut is that things are totally fucked up and can't be fixed. I'm not sure why, but I've always been able to talk to Joe. Whenever we've needed help on the road, Joe's been there. Whenever we've needed to get a song on the air or a show booked, Joe never lets us down.

He's happy to see me, but when he tells me where to meet him, my heart stops beating.

"1790 Broadway on the eighteenth floor. Roulette Records."

Oh shit.

Roulette Records is Morris Levy, the guy who put up the money for Sugar Hill. He's the guy they talk about at the office, but who nobody really knows.

The word on this cat is serious as a heart attack. Word is he's connected, and not to stick-up kids and hardrocks, like the thugs in the South Bronx, but to real-life gangsters. Maybe that's why this guy's got millions of dollars. Maybe that's why they say he can get anything done in the music business. Maybe that's why he's rolling the bank on the Queen.

I've heard some stuff on Mister Levy, especially since I've been sniffing around about publishing rights and other business that concerns me. The stuff is about guys like Frankie Lymon, Chuck Berry, and Tommy James . . . guys who wrote some monster hits. Guys who made Mister Levy all that money, but who don't have a dime to their own names.

My guess is that he's heard stuff about me too. Stuff about how I got a lawyer. Stuff about how I have reporter friends over at the New York *Daily News* and the *Boston Globe* and all over the country. Guys who I've been talking to about what's going on over at Sugar Hill.

My first thought is that I never should have stirred shit up. Might have had a chance to make things right if I had played along. Next, I go half out of my mind wondering whether they'll come looking for me if I don't make it to the meeting. Smoking coke won't help—I'll only get more paranoid. I'm not threatening anybody and I haven't asked for shit, though, so,I maintain.

But if this is just a talk, then what's Morris Levy got to do with it?

Better I face the music than run away, so the next morning I'm at the Roulette offices, staring at Mister Mo Levy. Me and Joe are sitting on the couch. Mister Levy is behind his desk. He's gotta be six inches taller than me. Stocky. And thick too; thick neck, thick arms, and thick hands. Fists like canned hams. He's got dead eyes like a thug. When he speaks, his voice sounds like sandpaper and his accent is heavy on the downtown. But he's smiling, and what he says catches me out of left field.

"It's great to finally meet you. I can't tell you how much I appreciate what you've done for our label."

Huh?

"Flash," Mr. Levy says, "do you like horses?"

"They're alright, I guess."

"Well, I love horses," Mr. Levy says. "Beautiful creatures. You care for them right and they'll love you to death. Give 'em a place to run, a good stable, feed 'em well, breed 'em right, and they'll give you everything they've got, especially the champions."

What's this cat saying?

"Thing is, they also know when they aren't being treated right. And while they might not be the smartest animals on the planet, they got instinct. Like a good whore—maybe she doesn't know the business, but she knows who wants to fuck her."

Mr. Levy smiles. Joe laughs. I just listen.

"I think of Sugar Hill Records as a champion's stable, and you and the Furious Five are the best thing we got going. But we understand that you're upset. And if you're upset, we're upset."

"Flash," Joe jumps in, "what can we do to make things right?"

I know what I *don't* want. "I don't want to fight anymore."

"Nobody wants that," Joe continues.

"I want out of my contract," I say.

But Joe doesn't say anything.

Mr. Levy answers instead. "What can we do to work this out?"

"I want out of the contract. This just doesn't feel right anymore."

I look at Joe and he looks at me. I can see that he's got pain in his heart over this situation. I can see he wants to do right by me. And I believe that if he could, he would.

But I can't get Sylvia's words outta my head.

"Flash is just a DJ ... we don't need him ..."

I know I don't want things to stay like they are, but the Queen's never gonna change her tune.

Mister Levy tells me to take some time to think it over. I leave the office, lost in my thoughts, trying to make sense of what just happened. Normally, I'd take the FDR up to the Willis Avenue Bridge if I'm comin' back from the City. Today, I take Lenox Ave. all the way up to 165th and then head east to Broadway.

Before I know it, I'm in front of the Audubon. It's been almost four years since I've been back.

The joint's all boarded up. Last I heard they don't rent it out for concerts anymore. Heard the rap shows just got too wild—kids breaking stuff, tearing the place apart, and not giving a fuck.

Now it's trashed up and shut down.

Takes all I got to keep from crying. Am I being boarded up and shut down?

Can't go back.
Can't stay here.
Don't know what I'm gonna do.

In that moment, I know that no matter how much I ask for, no matter what they offer me, Sylvia and them are never gonna let me do things my way with my group.

Like it or not, there's no future for me at Sugar Hill Records.

HOLE IN MY SOUL

ME: "What the fuck you mean, you want out?"

     HER: "I don't want to be with you anymore."

The "HER" is Paulette Two, a.k.a. Sweet Pea, and the "ME" is sweating bullets. "I want out" is the last thing I wanna hear right about now. I'll be the first one to say I've been a lousy boyfriend in every way, but I never thought it would come to this.

So I backpedal.

ME: "You know how much I love you."

HER: "That's bullshit, Flash."

ME: "What do you mean, bullshit?! My life's falling apart and you wanna come at me, talking about how you want out? Right when I need you most?"

HER: "See, that's what I'm talking about. You need me like you need that coke. Like you need all those other girls you're with. Lying to me. Having me lay up at night, after you say you're coming over. Now you're trying some guilt trip shit? I don't think so, Flash. I've had enough."

Now I'm getting scared.

Never seen my Sweet Pea this mad before. I've seen some fire come out of her mouth, but there's something in her voice this time that I've never heard before. Something stone dead. Something definite. When

I speak again, I can hear desperation in my voice and feel it in my stomach.

ME: "Wasn't always how you felt. We used to be good to each other. Remember? We can be good again."

HER: "I don't know, Flash. I don't know."

There it is again. That feeling like no matter what I say, nothing's gonna change her mind. But I don't give up.

ME: "I know I got it in me to be that man for you."

HER: "I don't think so. That man was Joseph. Flash ain't Joseph."

She's right. Joseph was a guy who experimented with the beats 'cause he loved 'em. Joseph was that nerdy poindexter who gave everything else up for the things he loved. But Flash is larger than life . . . hers *or* mine.

HER: "I don't give a fuck about Flash. I only cared about Joseph. I cared about the guy who played music. I cared about the man who didn't play me for cash-money, hos, and cocaine. You haven't been that man for a long time."

ME: "You're the only girl I love."

But that isn't really true . . . and she knows it.

ME: "You're the only one who can save me."

But deep down inside, I don't want to be saved.

ME: "I'll change for you . . . I'll do what it takes to make this work."

At this point, I'm saying anything.

HER: "Flash . . . I got another man."

I don't have a comeback for that one.

ME: "Who is he?"

HER: "Somebody you don't know. He's in the military. He's moving to Europe and I'm going with him."

The truth crushes my heart. Just like that, Paulette Jeffrey is gone, with nothing but her words echoing in my ears and burning in my chest.

HER: "Don't call me."

HER: "Don't come around my way."

HER: "I don't want to see you anymore."

I wish I could take the high road. Wish I could let her go gracefully. But I can't help it; I need her too much.

And the feelings I got are just way too big.

So I do the only thing I know—I get high.

I call up Bonita. (Not her real name.) Bonita's a girl I just met who likes the get-high as much as me. She's cool like that, but she's not Paulette.

I don't feel anything in Bonita's soul like I felt with my Sweet Pea.

That's okay.

As long as I'm high, I'm feeling the same way.

As long as I'm high, I'm filling the hole in my soul.

"WHITE LINES"

November 1983.

Stuck in a hole.

I'm back in the Bronx, holed up with my so-called girlfriend on 183rd and Bathgate, in a dingy hole of an apartment, 'cause I can't stay anyplace else. This is why: A couple months back, right after the thing with Mo and Joe, the guys called me up for another trip over to England.

"It's sixty large for two-and-a-half weeks of shows," Rahiem told me. "Cash doesn't come any easier than that. But the money isn't as good without you."

"We can do what we want afterwards," said Creole, "but don't be dumb here, Flash. Let's get paid."

"I can't, guys. I'm sorry, but . . . I just can't."

When Creole said what he said about doing what we want, he was talking about leaving the group. Creole and Rahiem and I have talked about doing our own thing at another label. And in the midst of all this drama, another label offered us all the stuff Sugar Hill never did. They said yes to publishing, yes to mechanical rights, and yes to a bunch of other stuff. They even bought us brand-new cars . . . not just for me and Creole and Rahiem, but for everybody—as bad as things are, I'm rolling around NYC in a brand-new BMW.

But when the plan to leave started getting serious, the Queen made legal moves of her own against us. Said the label owned our professional names and got a bunch of lawyers to make it sound legal. Morton Berger said we could fight it. The new label was behind us. But the Queen told the guys if we tried to leave, we'd leave with nothing.

The guys got scared.

Now I'm right back at square one, trying to get the guys to leave Sugar Hill.

In the meantime, my dignity won't let me put any more money in the Queen's pocket. So I said no to the tour. But when I said no, the guys asked my friend E-Z Mike to step up and DJ in my place, and he said yes.

Damn. When it rains, it pours.

I knew Mike was having problems of his own, but hearing that he'd do me like that hurt just as bad as losing Sweet Pea. It led to a big fight. And while I have fights on the regular with my groupmates, my sisters, and the moms of my kids, I can't ever remember the last time I had one with Mike.

So now I'm living in this hole with Bonita.

I'm also in the hole financially. I'm totally dead-ass broke. Haven't played a show in months—not even at Disco Fever—and I can't even remember the last time I laid my hands on the turntables. I'm flipping my possessions for pennies on the dollar, doing whatever it takes to get by. If the phone rings, I take it for granted it's somebody I owe money, so I don't answer it, even though it might be Paulette One or Jean, telling me the babies are asking for Daddy. Even though it might be Penny or Lilly, telling me Mom's having another bad spell. When the thought creeps in that I can't be there for my family, it makes me low—lower than anything. The low puts me back in another hole, an all-too-familiar one these days, one I can't get out of—the hole in the pipe.

I wanna fill it. Wanna plug it up. But I can't. And I can't stop feeling it. These days, I'm smoking to keep my head above water. The base doesn't get me high anymore, it just gets me even with the day. But it's the only thing that keeps me from going out of my mind, so I keep smoking.

The more I smoke, the further I fall into the hole in my soul.

———

Late November 1983.

Think it's a Monday.

Bonita's screaming in my ear that we're all out of cocaine. The phone's ringing, my heart's pounding, and all the holes in my life are emptier than they've ever been.

At least we still got a TV, which I'm watching while I wait for JB to arrive. JB's my DJ pal over at Disco Fever, but he also moves big weight on the street, and most important, he's my bottom-dollar hookup. Even when Paulette Two was telling every dealer around what she was gonna do if they sold to me, JB always came through. And even now that I'm broke, he still fronts me the purest flakes he's got.

Please let that phone call be JB.

On the screen, Nancy Reagan's talking about some new "Just Say No" antidrug thing. Telling kids to "just say no" if their friends try to pass 'em some drugs. Talking about how recreational drug use leads to hard addiction. Gotta wonder if Nancy Reagan knows what's going on in the real world.

My head starts to spin again. I'm wondering whether I should have just said no to the Queen. Wondering where I'd be if I'd just said no to Mel and the fellas when she bum-rushed us to sign with Sugar Hill. Wondering whether we would have got a better deal somewhere else. Wondering if I hadn't been such a bastard to Paulette One, Two, or Jean—or any of the girls I've ever loved for that matter—whether I could've had a shot. A shot at a normal life, a shot at happiness, or a shot at a little peace.

Bonita comes in the room. By the look in her eyes, I can already tell something's wrong.

"Tell me that was JB," I say.

"JB's dead," she says, laying it out there like a rug. My first thought isn't how, or why, or if his family is okay. My first thought is exactly what comes out of my mouth.

"How the fuck we gonna get high?"

Word is JB was tortured to death. They found him bound and gagged and dead in his bathtub, his girl next to him, done the same way.

Gotta think. But I gotta get high to think.

I get an idea. My boy KD (not his real name) is always down for the get-high and I know he'll have a connection. It takes me the rest of the day to track him down. My search leads me to another hole, this one over on 127th and St. Nicholas. His crib is scary.

It's another subterranean shit-trap with nothing but a grimy stair-case leading down and a red lightbulb to identify the joint. Down below, somebody's screaming and somebody else is laughing. Up on the street, bodies dart through the shadows and linger in the cut. I get a feeling I'm being watched, and a stronger feeling somebody's gonna set me off if I stay out here too long.

The dealers on the street . . .

The baggies in the gutter . . .

This isn't a place people come to live; the sun's going down and there isn't a lit window to be seen on the whole block.

The only thing people come here to do is smoke base.

I have a brief moment of sanity that goes something like, *Don't do this, Flash. Call Penny. Call Rahiem or Creole. Shit, call the cops if you have to, but whatever you do, do* not *walk down those steps.*

Then I hear it something like this:

VOICE 1: "Hey you wanna cop some blow?"

VOICE 2: "Sure, man, what you got, dust, flakes, or rocks?"

VOICE 1: "Man, I got China white, mother of pearl, ivory flake . . . what you need?"

VOICE 2: "Well, lemme check it out, lemme just get a little freeze . . ."

I spin around to see who all's behind me, but it's just one kid in a red leather Michael Jackson jacket, a boom box at his feet, hustling dope. He's looking out for the cops with one eye and looking out for paying customers with the other.

"Who said that?" I ask him.

He points at the radio. "New Grandmaster Flash jam."

Can't be.

Nobody told me.

Morton Berger said they can't use my name until our case settles.

I think it must be some kind of mistake.

I ask the kid to show me the cassette tape.

The kid ain't lying.

SUGAR HILL RECORDS
"WHITE LINES"
(Sylvia Robinson/Melvin Glover)
GRANDMASTER FLASH
and the FURIOUS FIVE

I hear the chorus. I'd recognize those voices anywhere.

Sugar Hill house band backing vocalists.

Singin' about . . .

White lines . . . running through my mind . . .

Then I hear Mel's voice. He's rapping about cocaine. Rapping about snorting it, shooting it, smoking it . . .

How it's sweet as sugar and bitter as salt.

Rapping about, "Don't do it!"

Shhhhhiiiit.

Don't do it?

Everybody's doing it!

Everybody's off in their own little world, doing white lines. Sniffing all their money up their nose. Killing their brains. Now the guys are saying no to drugs on this new record, but I bet they're out looking for the dope man just like me.

The song's one big hypocritical joke.

But the more it's talkin' 'bout white lines, the more my mouth starts to water.

White lines . . .

Then I get the shakes.

Running through my mind . . .

Then my skin starts to itch.

I forget about everything I got in my life that's good.

I don't walk—I *run* down those stairs.

I run right down into . . .

hell

Soon as I step through the door, I can smell it.

    I know it's ether, but when it burns with the coke, it smells like ammonia or chlorine or some kind of disinfectant.

I can feel it burning my lungs. The fumes are so heavy in the air, it stings—makes the muscles in my chest seize up. Feels like I'm breathing lead. Even though I should be used to the smell, here in hell the foul stink has me choking.

I hear the gurgle of water pipes and Bics flicking. I hear KD's base-head friends breathing deep. I hear the sound of vials and baggies on the floor: crinkling, crunching, cracking, coming apart beneath my feet when I step inside.

There's a ratty lamp in the corner—a single bulb, attached to an extension cord that hangs through a mucky, rotten hole in the ceiling. On the other side of the place, a dying fluorescent bulb gives me a glimpse of the world's filthiest bathroom. When the bulb flickers, I see silhouettes of bodies in the hall: knees up, shoulders hunched, lips suckin' on those little glass dicks like there was honey, God, and peace on earth comin' through the other end.

I get low so the burning vapor doesn't hurt so bad—gotta be why everybody's down on the floor here—but the smells coming up from the carpet are even worse. Some of these devils urinate and shit where they post up and they haven't moved for days. Just flick, suck . . . hold it in . . . breathe it out . . . and drift away.

I can dig it. All I care about at this moment is the get-high. It's been almost twelve hours since I had anything to smoke and my skin's starting to crawl. When I look down, I got goose bumps, and I know it won't be long before they start to itch beneath the surface.

I look around and see a dealer in the corner. I buy a half a quarter of rock already cooked up and ready to go.

I look down. There, at my feet, is a funky, skin-and-bones white dude, hair matted and clumpy. He's got hollow eyes, sores on his cheeks, and his skin's so greasy I can see his pipe glowing in the oils on his forehead. This dude is so tore-up and smelly, my stomach turns.

The dealer shows me to a private room in the back and hands me a torch made out of a wire hanger with gauze at the tip. Then he passes me rubbing alcohol so I can dip, light, and blast off.

Flick . . . suck . . . AHHHHHHHHHHHHHHHH . . .

I slide down the wall, collapsing into a heap.

Flick . . . suck . . . AHHHHHHHHHHHHHHHHHHHHHHHH . . .

As I take the next hit from my pipe, the room begins to spin, and I fall into a dream.

———

I'm lying in a field of cool, tall grass.

Don't know how I got here. Don't know if it's real.

But at least I got a moment's peace.

I can feel the blades against my face and the cool dew against my back. The weight of the chemical fumes in my chest is a distant memory. Instead, my lungs are filled with the sweet aroma of morning country air.

Must be early summer. The air is crisp, but I can already tell it's going to be a warm day.

Suddenly I feel the touch of a soft hand.

"Butsy . . ."

It's a little voice. One that's very familiar. But one that I haven't heard in a very long time.

"Butsy!"

I look to my right and there's Lilly, holding my hand. Not the young woman I saw a couple months ago, squealing about how her brother was gonna be on Soul Train. *This is the Lilly I remember from 1969. This is a little girl of eight.*

"Where are we, Butsy?"

"That's easy. We're up here at the Greer School. Upstate. Out in the meadow where we used to pick berries."

She's staring up at the sky with eyes so big, they might float right out of her head.

"No, we aren't, Butsy. No, we aren't."

"Of course we are ... we're up here at Greer and it's just like it always was. We ain't got no problems and nothing to worry about."

Then she turns her head and looks at me.

Suddenly, the hole in my soul fills my chest. Fills it with that terrible weight that pulls me back down.

Everything is NOT okay.

Everything around me becomes cold and dark. An icy chill travels through my veins and burrows into my bones.

Now I'm falling.

Don't know what's up.

Don't know what's down.

Don't know where I'm going and I don't know where I've been. I'm lost in the dark for what feels like forever. But then I see a glimmer of hope and a small twinkle of light in the inky blackness.

A trapdoor, but it's so far away ... and I can't stop falling through space.

I'm truly doomed if I don't try ...

Think I can make it ...

I do ...

Open the door and fall into darkness ...

The next thing I know I hear a voice.

"Flash," the voice says, but it comes from outside my dream.

"Flash," the voice repeats my name. I know this voice.

"Wake up, Flash," insists the same voice. "You gotta wake up. You gotta get out of here. I'll help you, but you gotta help me too."

I open my eyes and see my sister.

"I love you, Flash," says Penny, "and I'm not going to let you die."

Part Five

life after death

Keep the beat, don't ever let it end . . .

—Rakim

INBORN

Penny saved me.

I don't know how long I was in and out of that basement down on St. Nicholas, but it felt like almost a year. By some miracle, my beautiful big sister found me right when I overdosed, dragged me out, and took me to St. Barnabas Hospital. When I finally opened my eyes, there she was. Crying tears of anger, relief, and joy.

By then, it was almost 1985.

I'd been in a coma for two days. I needed eight quarts of saline to get me rehydrated. I had blisters on my lips and fingers from pipes and lighters. Thanks to a steady diet of nothing but smoking coke for months on end, my teeth were a mess and I weighed 118 pounds. That meant I couldn't eat solid foods, so they put a tube up my nose. I was too weak to move, and with all the time in the world, I had nothing to do but think.

I was ashamed of how I'd done my family, my friends, and my gift. I regretted what had happened in my career and was disgusted with myself for not having handled my business better. I was in despair that I'd never have passion like I did with Paulette Jeffrey, and I was terrified Paulette Dawson and Jean wouldn't ever let me see my kids again. Worst of all, I had no idea what to do about any of it.

Those were dark and lonely hours, and I didn't have much to say. Through it all, Penny never left my side and mercifully respected my silence, waiting for me to make the first move, knowing that eventually I would speak.

"I don't know what I'm gonna do, P."

"That's easy. You're gonna spin records, just like you always have."

"Won't be like it was," I lamented. "Everything's different now."

"Then you roll with it, put your hands where you know they belong, and start all over again."

I knew what she was getting at. And I thought about what it would take to lay my fingers back on the turntables as I struggled to tie my shoes. I'd been running in a drug-induced blackout for almost a year; now, sitting on the edge of my hospital bed, trying to figure out whether I needed to loop the lace to the right or the left, I seriously wondered whether I'd smoked up my ability to keep the beat.

Keeping the beat was the least of my problems. First and foremost, I had no idea how to live like a normal human being. Between the circus that had been my life as Grandmaster Flash and the hell that had been my existence as a basehead, even tying my shoes was an accomplishment. Back in the day when I first broke my skills at the clubs, gyms, and dancehalls, people would stop what they were doing to watch me spin. They would actually stop dancing, stop scamming and thugging on one another, form a crowd around my DJ tables, and watch me do my thing. Now I'd watch normal people do normal things in a normal way and I couldn't figure anything out for the life of me.

Paying the bills.

Getting to work on time.

Making a bed.

Washing a dish.

Keeping a dentist's appointment.

You might as well have asked me to fly a plane; it all seemed too much to handle.

All I had were the clothes on my back and what was left of my records and gear. At first, I went up to Bonita's place, thinking I could get back in there, even though she still wanted to get high. Thought maybe she'd see things my way and give the pipe a rest, but she didn't.

HER: "Where you been?"

ME: "Nobody told you?"

HER: "Told me what?"

ME: "I almost died."

HER: "*Died?* What from?"

ME: "Smoking that rock."

HER: *"Damn."* She was quiet for a minute. "But you okay *now,* right?"

As soon as she said that, I knew we were moving in opposite directions. When she looked at me and asked if I was okay—out of the corner of her eye and with a frown—I knew she wasn't asking about my health, she was asking if I was good to get high. And just like I knew what was up, Bonita knew she wasn't getting the old Flash back. It wasn't shady on her part—she didn't try to talk me back in the dope game and I didn't try to talk her out of it—but Bonita went her way and I went mine.

My new way meant moving in with Penny down on 146th and St. Anne's and starting to pull my own weight. On Tuesdays, Penny gave me a grocery list, fronted me some money, and shoved me out the door. Once I was at the supermarket, I'd go up and down the aisles like I was lost, not knowing what was money well spent and what wasn't. Not knowing how much stuff I could carry home with two hands. Not knowing what to buy so I could make pancakes. It's a bitch; the little things in life don't seem small when you're starting over again from scratch.

At twenty-three, I was flexed. At twenty-eight, I was taking the train. Waiting on the platform, the smell of the subway was nothing like the smell of leather and wood in a new car, or jet fuel out on the runway while boarding a private plane. Leather and jet fuel were long gone. Now it was the smell of soot, stale air, and piss.

Now I was a citizen. I didn't buy a new suit when the old one got wrinkled. I didn't have a girl to wash my stuff for me. Barely even had stuff to wear. I punched quarters in a machine, mixed in the detergent, dropped my clothes in the hole, and watched 'em spin around in the window. *Punch, mix, drop, spin ... day in and day out.*

I slept on my sister's couch and tried to be grateful I was alive. Sounds simple enough now, but at the time it was impossible. Pushing a grocery cart at the market and trying to remember to pick up the frozen peas wasn't filling the hole in my soul. But I knew cocaine wouldn't fill it either. So I kept doing what I was doing and living a very small life.

By late 1985, I had two ties to the rap game. One was the legal battle with Sylvia Robinson and Sugar Hill over the ownership of my identity.

Sugar Hill had still been printing copies of "White Lines" as recorded by Grandmaster Flash and the Furious Five. Sugar Hill also claimed to own the words "Grandmaster" and "Flash" and said that I couldn't use them together for any reason. The case was pending, but the long and short of it was that I was fighting for my own name.

The other tie to the rap game was the radio, but the radio didn't sound like it used to. Somewhere, something about the music had changed.

Run DMC was on top. They'd been on the move for the past two years and represented the new style. Run DMC kept it true to the old school—MCs and a DJ performing together—but their lyrics and their image made it clear that a new era was taking over.

Even if it was different, I loved those guys, especially Jam Master Jay. When I heard what he could do with a couple of turntables, it made me proud. But still, I wasn't hearing DJs getting put up the way they used to. Rap was bigger than ever, but I was starting to worry about the art form I loved so much.

Hip hop was starting to go mainstream, and it was leaving its roots behind. Hollywood was pimping it with movies like *Breakin'* and *Beat Street*, but the DJs weren't out on the corner, at the park or the gyms, the way we used to be. The ghetto blaster had replaced the sound system and the mix tape had replaced the live set. Crack was hitting the streets hard and hardly anybody threw block parties anymore.

Block parties and the club flavor was gone from the Bronx. Disco Fever and all the old spots were closing down. "There's no club money in the Bronx anymore, Flash." That was Sal Abbatiello talking, my man who'd put me up all those years at the Fever. If he was telling me it was the end of an era, I believed it. "It was all good back when downtown had to come uptown. But things changed. People started getting killed."

Damn. Was Disco Fever shutting down for good?

"Russell Simmons and a bunch of guys from Hollywood filmed a movie at the club and the city closed our doors for good," Sal explained. "Said we didn't have our performance permits in order. Can you believe that shit? After all those years, doing like we did?"

Suddenly I felt like Herc. Felt like the Cold Crush Brothers and Caz. Felt left behind.

The Bronx was my home.

The Bronx was where I did my thing.

But somehow, the Bronx had been left behind.

"I wish I could do something for you, Flash," Sal said. "You're like family to me. But if you want to play hip hop, you're better off in Manhattan."

Maybe I could go into the City. Maybe I could spin records downtown. But did I want to? Somewhere along the way, the heart and soul of what I had helped to create had disappeared. Downtown was up, uptown was down, and I was about to see a movie that would take everything I felt and spin it on its ear.

One night in November of 1985, I found myself in a dark Harlem theater watching *Krush Groove*, the Russell Simmons movie Sal was talking about.

Krush Groove was a story about rap, but it was really a story about getting paid. Knowing how to get paid. Knowing how to *stay* paid. Knowing how to deal with crooked big-time record label owners and beat 'em at their own game. Yeah, Run DMC was up there on the screen. Yeah, there was Kurtis Blow, holding it down from the old days. The Fat Boys were carefully crafting their image as the Three Stooges of rap, and LL Cool J, the boy-wonder from Queens, walked into the casting call like King Kong, banged on his chest, and spit out brilliant rhymes like he had a buzz saw stuck in his throat. I even got to see the white kids everybody had been talking about, the Beastie Boys, and they had game.

But none of those guys was what the movie was really about. *Krush Groove* was about Russell Simmons, his real-life record label called Def Jam. *Krush Groove* was about how to take it to the next level … about how to do everything me and the Five didn't do.

I got home that night and the hole in my soul got bigger. I hardly said a word at the dinner table.

"You're not eating," Penny finally said. "So spit it out. What's eating you?"

"I don't know, P."

"You went to see that movie today, didn't you? I hear they give you a shout."

"Yeah," I mumbled. "They mention me. But the phone ain't ringing."

Penny looked at me and smiled. "Remember when you was little? I mean *real* little? So little that you couldn't even stand up?"

"Not really."

"Well I *do*," she continued. "Dad would throw on 'I'm Walking' by Fats Domino and you'd go nuts. You'd put your hands out in front of you and make 'em go around and around like you was cutting. Before there ever was such a thing. Before you had invented it."

Hearing somebody else say it felt good, even if it was my sister.

I had invented something.

Still smiling, she continued: "You had a big grin on your little face, and your tiny fingers would be going back and forth, like you thought you was making the beat go bop. We couldn't figure it out, but we'd watch you do it for hours."

As Penny continued to reminisce, I thought back to crawling out of the crib just to be near the music. Long before I found girls and drugs, beats were the high.

"After Dad split, I watched you make a record play with a sewing needle. God only knows how you knew to do that. And when you couldn't get anyone to help you spin the record, you would just put your head on the floor to listen to the neighbors' jams downstairs. You'd come to the dinner table and the whole side of your face would be filthy with dust. Mom would lose her damn mind and start screamin' 'bout how she was gonna smack you clean ... You'd wash up, but as soon as the table was cleared, you was right back down on the ground, getting your face ashy all over again."

I *did* remember it and I laughed.

Then Penny stopped smiling. Dead serious, she said, "We all knew you had it in you to make something out of nothing, something great."

Penny paused, then looked me straight in the eye: "What you do, boy, is inborn. It's your gift. No one and nothing can take it away from you, but ain't no one and nothing can get you back in the game. Only you can do that."

EMOTIONAL BEATDOWN

Krush *Groove* and Penny's words had me going. Couldn't stop thinking about Run DMC, Rick Rubin, Russell Simmons, and the rap game.

I fixated on Russell. He was called Rush by his friends, and with good reason; my man had been born to get his hustle on. I had seen his face in the crowd dozens of times back in the day. He'd be back in the cut, while everybody else was dancing. He'd be watching the MCs, but he'd be watching the crowd first. He'd also be watching whoever was collecting the money.

When he started pushing parties out in Queens and over at Fordham University, it was 1982. Me and the Five were already white-hot. By then, all I cared about was getting paid, and the last thing I wanted was another promoter nipping at my heels, trying to grind me on my price to rock a show. But there he was, just as tenacious and scrappy as he wanted to be, never taking no for an answer.

Russell also always had his younger brother, Joe, and Joe's best friend, Daryl, with him. Those guys couldn't have been two years out of junior high when I first heard 'em rap. They looked out of place in their plaid jackets and hats, nobody was rocking, but when they took the stage at Disco Fever and started rapping, everybody shut up. You had to give 'em mad respect; Run DMC knew how to absolutely wreck a crowd with two turntables and a microphone.

While Grandmaster Flash and the Furious Five went off to conquer the world, Run DMC and Russell stayed home and paid their dues. While they came up through the ranks, Russell made sure nobody played funny games with their money. Russell also made sure the money came through him, and he made sure the checks cleared. And while the rappers were cultivating their styles and rhymes, Russell was paying attention to the music business. Russell was taking notes, aiming all the while to go into business for himself.

Krush Groove was a mirror of the real Russell. He was rubbing two nickels together to make a dime, borrowing from Peter to pay Paul, and doing all the legwork while his brother got all the juice. Russell was reading contracts. Cutting records. Taking orders and shipping 12-inch singles. Doing all of it out of a one-room office that doubled as a crash pad he split with Rick Rubin, the caveman-white-boy-genius who made those early records sound so incredible.

But that was a year and a half ago. Now Russell and Rick were building up the Def Jam stable and changing the face of rap. Actually, Def Jam *was* rap. Sugar Hill was in bad shape and the majors were still trying to figure out how to get in on the scene. A lot of folks still said rap music was a fad, but Russell and them knew better, and by the time he had Run DMC headlining Fresh Fest in 1984 (while a very young Jermaine Dupri was break dancing off to the side of the stage), nobody watching the show would argue—rap was here to stay.

Back in the day, I wouldn't have traded places with Russell Simmons for all the vinyl in the Bronx. Back in the day, my life was easy while he had to fight for everything he had. But now I had nothing and he had it all. Word was he had just signed a distribution deal worth millions. I would give anything to be in his shoes.

Why couldn't I be Russell Simmons? Why couldn't I have my own record company? I knew how to make records. I knew good rappers from bad. Maybe I didn't know the business back in the day, but I could learn it now. I could take classes and read books. I could learn to pay myself like Russell did, and then I could get a second chance at the game.

Besides, Sylvia and Joe hadn't had a hit in years and were up to their back teeth in debt. I was thinking, maybe I could go to Mo Levy . . . maybe I could start signing rappers myself. Maybe I could run my own label and get guys from the old days—guys like Ray Chandler and E-Z Mike and Disco Bee—to help me out. We'd take over and show everybody how to do it.

But I was just fooling myself.

I didn't see Ray too often. We were cool, but he wasn't a nine-to-five guy any more than I was. Bee had his own thing going on. As for my best friend, Mike ended up loving his drugs even more than I did; he'd caught a case somewhere along the way and landed in jail.

Mo Levy had cashed out of Sugar Hill and was being indicted by the feds. Even if he didn't have problems of his own, he wouldn't have given me a crumb. Who was I kidding? I didn't know a soul who would take a chance on me.

I wasn't going back to school.

I didn't even have a bank account.

I never got anything but cheated in the music business.

To think it was going to change now was crazy.

"No one and nothing can get you back in the game but you."

It was late after dinner that night, but Penny's words kept ringing in my ears, just as my daydreams of reclaiming lost success were swimming through my brain. As I lay on the couch, waiting for sleep to come, I started feeling everything at once: envy, anger, resentment, fear, confusion, guilt—all of it screaming at me.

All of it telling me I was on the outside and there was no room for me at the table.

I was feeling bad for feeling bad. I was mad at myself 'cause I couldn't let it go. I was wondering what was wrong with me that I couldn't have just done a little coke and handled my business. I was calling myself a dummy 'cause I wasn't Russell Simmons.

I was pissed at my group and so-called friends, but wondering if I had the right to be. I was pissed at the ladies in my life, but admitted that I hadn't always done right by them. I was wishing I'd had a mom I could talk to, but she was more troubled than ever. I was wishing my dad had been around more.

Lying there in the dark, I might not have been in hell anymore, but I was slowly going nuts.

What if things never got any better?

WHAT'S IN A NAME?

The phone woke me up the next morning.

"Flash. It's Morton Berger. Judge Brient wants us downtown tomorrow morning. Nine A.M. And Flash? Wear a suit."

By now, Joseph Saddler and Sylvia Robinson had been fighting over who owned the name "Grandmaster Flash" for over a year. There'd been rehearsals on how to behave, what to say, and what not to say with Creole, Rahiem, and me—how to be stone-faced and not show emotion. There'd been moments where it looked like Mel, Scorp, and Cowboy might come correct on our side, but then they stopped showing up and stopped returning phone calls. All I heard from the Robinsons and their people was that I was a useless crackhead and a useless DJ.

But Morton Berger's phone call meant Judge Brient had made a decision on the issue.

My name.

Grandmaster Flash.

Like it could belong to anybody else but me. Like anybody else could have done what I did. Like anybody else could claim my place in history. The fact that a judge could decide all that only got me angrier.

That's what was roaring through my head like a four-alarm fire, making my emotional hangover even worse as soon as the phone hit the cradle. This legal battle was real, and it had me asking a whole other level of questions.

Would I ever own the name Grandmaster Flash?

Was my name ever mine to begin with?

I never questioned that I was who I was, or that I'd created what I'd created. But my name was given to me by two separate people—my childhood friends Gordon Upshaw and Joe Kidd. A dozen or more helped me build it up over the years. Did they own a piece of me too? Am I supposed to be paying somebody else their dues for my name?

I walked to Fordham Road to buy a suit and the questions persisted. What did my name mean? What did it stand for? Was it about parties and clubs? Photo shoots and trashing hotel rooms? Was it about catching cases and being chased by helicopters? Was it about getting high and getting laid? When I heard the words "Grandmaster" and "Flash" together, did I see dollars or did I see turntables? Did I see groupies and drug dealers? Did I see legal troubles or a way to feed my kids?

Did I see good or bad?

Did I see darkness or light?

I went to the barbershop for a fade and my mind kept spinning. What did Grandmaster Flash mean to the faces in the crowd? Did it mean you were about to be served by the baddest DJ you'd ever known? Or did it make you scratch your head and say, "Whatever happened to that guy?"

Was Grandmaster Flash still somebody who mattered?

Did Flash matter or was it time to be Joseph Saddler?

Who *was* Joseph anyway? Was he just a kid from Dewey Avenue? Was he somebody's brother, son, dad, or best friend? Was Joseph a scientist who needed to return to the lab? Was it time to retreat back down into his basement, like the one he had over on Faille Street back in the Bronx, where it was just him and his experiments? Where he could come up with something new all over again? Was it time for Joseph to reinvent himself? Find some new style of spinning records? Did Joseph have it in him to be a pioneer all over again?

Sitting at Penny's table that night, eating food I hadn't paid for, I thought about tomorrow and wondered what my name was worth. What was it worth on paper? What was it worth on the streets? What was it worth to my family? What was it worth to my kids? What was it worth to me?

After dinner, I threw on a few old slow jams for Penny that made me feel a little better about crashing at her place rent-free. But she picked up that my head was elsewhere and called me out.

"What's wrong, Butsy?"

"This case," I told her. "I don't know who or what I'm fighting for."

"You're fighting the bitch for ownership of your name, that's who and what you're fighting for," Penny reminded me. "You're a fighter, Butsy. You're pugnacious. That was one thing you got from our dad that was any good. You never gave up on anything in your life and as long as I'm around you never will."

Penny's words made me feel better, but after she went to bed, I got to thinking again and couldn't turn off my mind.

Didn't want to hate or hurt anyone.

But I also didn't want to keep running these stressful thoughts around in my brain.

So I just lay there on the couch, scared to move forward and scared to go back where I came from. Sweating what would happen if I lost. Sweating what would happen if I won. Sweating what kind of fool-headed shit I might say if I saw the Robinsons. Sweating what to do with my life, win or lose.

Would I become a citizen and let my beats die with me, or would I push forward? I finally slept.

I woke up the next morning and it was hard to get up off the couch. Was hard to put on my new suit. Didn't want to go. But I had to.

"It looks better if you're there," Morton Berger told me over the phone.

Looks better if I'm paying attention to my own business.

Looks better if I'm representing for myself.

Still, it was hard to make myself something to eat before Penny and I left out the door and caught the train into Lower Manhattan.

Penny and I sat and waited for hours for the case to come up. Sat and waited on a cold, hard bench outside that big, cold, empty courtroom in Lower Manhattan. Sat there wondering if my name was worth anything without rappers to back me up.

Didn't have an answer to that. Furthermore, it raised a bigger question . . .

Did DJs still matter?

Kept hearing the Queen's words echoing back to me: *He's just a*

DJ … we don't need him. Kept thinking about how it was the rapper, not the DJ, who took up the most space on the album covers these days.

Those thoughts came from the hole in my soul.

But somehow I still believed there was a place for DJs in the world.

Finally, it was time to face the music.

Stood in front of a judge. Me, Penny, Rahiem, Creole, and Morton Berger on one side, the Sugar Hill lawyer and the Robinsons on the other side. Then Mel came in and sat down behind the Robinsons. My heart sank.

Lastly, Judge Brient came in and sat down. Big silence. Big tension. Finally, he spoke. Said that on one hand, I didn't have a copyright on the words "Grandmaster" and "Flash" used together in the same sentence. Furthermore, the court hadn't seen any evidence of a clear legal contract that said what I owned and what Sugar Hill Records owned when it came to the business interests between us. But then the judge talked about the evidence we had submitted and explained in legalese the role I played in creating my name and branding it. It was all Greek to me; I was so confused I was almost crying.

After what seemed like forever and a day, Judge Brient said it was quite clear this musical marriage could not continue. And that much I knew.

"By law," he declared, "I am divorcing this situation."

BAM!

He struck the gavel.

BAM! Grandmaster Flash and Sugar Hill was no more.

When I looked at Morton Berger he was looking back at me, smiling ear to ear.

"What does all that mean?" I asked Morton.

"Means we won, Flash," he said. "Means you're free. They can still use the word 'Grandmaster,' but they can't use it together with the word 'Flash.' And Furious Five or no, it also means that now you can go after Sugar Hill Records for punitive damages. Emotional hardship. Pain and suffering. Say the word and I'll file the papers tomorrow morning. Just tell me what you want."

What I wanted.

Did I really want to go after Sugar Hill? Was the money gonna make me feel better? Was the money gonna heal the hurt and pain of breaking up the Furious Five? Was the money gonna get me back in the game?

"No," I told my lawyer. "All I want is my name."

My name.

I had my name.

What now?

What in hell was I gonna do with it? Before I turned out the lights that evening, I said a prayer. Didn't know to who or what—God, Jehovah, or Jesus—and didn't know where the prayer came from.

"I don't want to dream and I don't want to fade out," I whispered. "I don't want to ride this couch for the rest of my life. I don't want to go back to where I came from, and I don't want to be something I'm not. I just want to be Flash. I just want to be a DJ. I just want to play for someone. Don't care who or when or how or where. That's it, God. Thanks."

"THIS IS GRANDMASTER FLASH FLASH FLASH FLASH!"

I had my name back.

I could do whatever I wanted with it. I could record, I could play shows, I could print up "Grandmaster Flash for President" on a million T-shirts and sell 'em in Times Square if I felt like it.

Everybody kept telling me it was a big deal.

I was supposed to be happy but wasn't. Still felt like shit and didn't understand why. I was still angry at a lot of people and I still wanted to see 'em hurt. Mel was calling himself "Grandmaster Melle Mel" on his new records. Why would he do that? He already had the royalties and rights to all the music, why did he have to take half of my name too?

Still couldn't forgive those who'd taken from me what was mine. Thought I'd taken the high road when it came to not getting greedy with damages and more lawsuits, but that did nothing for me being pissed off.

Worst of all, I had a hunch that the pain, shame, anger, envy, fear, and confusion were all connected. Had a hunch I couldn't let go of hating myself unless I let go of hating others. But the hunch was buried down so deep, it was rarely more than a passing thought. It didn't take root and grow into something beautiful.

I see it looking back, but at the time I didn't know where to begin. And when in doubt, I did nothing. I might have prayed to God not to ride that couch but that's exactly what I did. Waited for the phone to ring. Waited for the deals to come to me. Didn't hustle a thing.

January 28, 1986.

I'd been riding the couch for a while. Penny was yelling at me to get out and get something—*anything*—by way of a job. I was watching TV when the news came that the space shuttle *Challenger* had exploded.

Horrible.

One second it was in flight, and the next it was a gigantic ball of fire. Seven lives extinguished in the blink of an eye. They said one of the astronauts was a teacher. I thought about all the lessons she'd never get to share, all the young people whose lives she'd never touch.

What was this short existence all about?

Now I *had* to get out of the apartment, so I went to Mott Haven Park. It was a cold day, but the air was so crisp in my lungs that I couldn't help but be glad I was still alive. The sun was out, shining on my face, and again, I found myself saying another prayer. "God, I know it could have been me who'd gone up in smoke. Thanks for that. But please show me what to do with it."

"Flash!"

It was Money Mike, another street kid from way-back-when who was grinding now, and by the look of it, he was coming up in a big way. Money had three gold chains as thick as my thumbs, new Adidas kicks, head-to-toe Fila, and in his pocket he had a bankroll so big it made his waistband sag.

"Haven't seen you in a fat minute. You still doin' it like you used to, Flash?"

"Nah. I'm straight," I said. Money was talking about blow. I could have easily asked for the hookup and he would have given it to me. I struggled with that thought and resisted.

"You still cutting those records like you used to?" he asked.

That was a better question. And the answer was yes. Penny was on my ass to spin as much as possible. I'd been getting back at it, but my hands were rusty, I wasn't up on hot jams, and my gear was raggedy.

Most of all, I had no audience.

"Yeah, I'm still spinnin'," I told him.

"If you're not smoking anymore, what do you want for one of those mix tapes?" Money asked.

Toward the end of my run, I'd copped coke from dealers in exchange for customized mix tapes. They'd give me an ounce or two and I'd mix up a ninety-minute DJ set, throwing the cat's name over an echo chamber every now and then, like: *This is Grandmaster FLASH FLASH FLASH FLASH ... Big EL EL EL EL ... This one's for YOU YOU YOU YOU!*" It wasn't a big deal for me, but to a cat from the streets who was trying to floss his rep, my name riding a jam next to his was big. I'd heard guys rolling through the Bronx, playing one of those tapes with their stereos cranked up so loud everybody knew they were down with me.

"For serious, Flash. I want a tape. How much?"

I'd been sweating a job recently. The only other one I'd ever had was at Crantex Fabrics, and I had to get paid, so this was an opportunity. I didn't want to be a drain on my sister; she had kids of her own. My kids had financial needs too. I didn't want to stay at Penny's forever. I needed a crib and I needed bread.

"Gimme a dollar a minute for the mix and don't copy the tape," I said. "If I ever find out you're bootlegging, I won't ever make another one for you."

Bootlegging a tape was a holdout rule of mine from the old days; I could only get paid for my efforts if you had to come to me for the goods. It worked out anyway; putting the cat's name on the tape meant I'd know who played me out. Long story short, Money was cool with the terms—and so was a business partner of his, who later that day asked for a tape of his own.

Now I had a job. Now I had a way to pay my bills. Can't say I was happy about it, though. I was back to taking requests. The phone would ring and somebody would say, "Flash, I want some 'Dance to the Drummer's Beat' mixed with 'Bongo Rock,' then I wanna slow it down with some 'T Plays It Cool' by Marvin Gaye and Sade ... then throw down some Janet Jackson in the mix, and make it all fresh."

It was like taking orders at a restaurant. I didn't take orders from anybody back when my name used to mean something. Now I was putting my ego aside so I could put up somebody else's name. It also bothered me that young brothers were using drugs and guns to get by rather than turntables and microphones. Bothered me that nobody was talking about it on wax.

Not that the rap scene wasn't still on the up and up. Run DMC was continuing to rule with "Walk This Way," the biggest hip hop jam ever produced. The song was all over MTV and had crossed over so big that white kids in Middle America were rocking it.

Don't get me wrong; I gave Run DMC mad respect for being real to who they were and still selling so many records, no question about it. But it bothered me that nobody was talking about black life in rap music. Now I don't judge anyone for how they choose to get over—either in the music business or on the street—but it didn't seem right that the place where it came from didn't have a voice. Right about then, it needed one bad.

As I ran the streets throughout 1986, I could see what Reaganomics was doing to the Bronx—the same thing Sugar Hill Records had done to me and my group. I'd hear the president talk about how the economy was supposed to be strong and people were supposed to be living large in America.

But none of that was happening in the Bronx.

If anything, the Bronx was getting worse. Worse than it had been in the days of the gangs. Worse than it had been in the summer of '77. Worse than ever. Crack had hit the streets so hard by then, how the hell was anybody supposed to "just say no"?

If there was a God, it was time for Him to say something. Well, it turns out He did.

One day I was playing records at a local store with Disco Bee and a couple of other friends when a kid wearing an Adelphi University jacket came through the door and said he had a jam we had to hear. Those days, seemed like everybody had a demo tape and most of 'em stunk, but this kid wouldn't stop talking about his.

"My man might be from Long Island, but he knows what he's doing. C'mon, Flash, play the tape."

I finally said yes just to shut him up . . . but man, was I glad I played it!

First thing I noticed was the DJ knew what he was doing. The jam opened over a killer cut of Fred Wesley's "Blow Your Head." Then came a high, scrappy hype man's voice talking up his main rapper. Soon as the lead vocal dropped in with a bang, I was hooked.

The lead MC began to rap. Not about how he made the ladies swoon or how fly he was, or how he could battle any other MC to the mat. This cat was all ideas.

Black America was asleep at the wheel.

Black America was being sold a false bill of goods.

Black America needed to stand up for itself; the rest of America wasn't going to give us anything for free.

In light of what I'd been through, I could dig it all.

What sold it all was his voice: it was a directive low tenor used like a battering ram. And though it wasn't anything I could put my finger on, something in his voice was so confident and strong that I knew this brother was for real. This wasn't some local kid kicking a toast or a party rhyme . . . this here was a *man*, and the man was saying something.

> *It was war they wanted and war they got,*
> *But they melted in the heat when my uzi got hot*

"Who the hell is this?" I asked the kid from Long Island.

"My man's name is Chuck D," he said, "and the squad's Public Enemy."

As 1986 rolled on, the music only got better. And deeper. The next group to come along that really blew my mind was KRS-One and Boogie Down Productions. Everything I saw on the streets of the Bronx, KRS saw too, because he was living on them, homeless. Rumor had it he was discovered in a shelter at the Franklin Armory, but rumor or not, the kid could rhyme. Boogie Down Productions, which was KRS and DJ Scott La Rock, made their name when they leveled a diss at MC Shan, then continued to put out music.

KRS was also telling people things nobody else did: don't smoke crack, stop making babies, stop committing black-on-black violence . . . and like Public Enemy had been saying from jump street, know your history. It all seemed so obvious, but it took on a new meaning coming through the speakerbox on the radio.

Now the Bronx had a rapper who told it like it was. He wasn't just saying that rap started here, he was giving new life to the place I called home. He was giving a voice to a place that rap had largely forgotten and telling the world that the Bronx still mattered. KRS wasn't a braggart about anything other than the knowledge he had to teach. But KRS didn't just teach it, he *preached* it. He put his ghetto reality right up under everybody's nose with a loud voice you couldn't ignore.

I loved it. I'd turn on the radio and I'd hear a new Boogie Down Productions jam and I'd fall in love with the music all over again.

Finally, there was Eric B. and Rakim.

I'd heard there was another group from Long Island—this one DJ and this one rapper—and they were supposed to be good ... *really* good. "Eric B. and Rakim's the best I ever heard," said my nephew, Ramel, after hearing their song at a party, but I didn't believe him until I heard them for myself.

Ramel wasn't exaggerating.

I would listen to "Eric B. Is President" a thousand times before I fully absorbed it, but it took only one play and I was sold.

First off, Eric B. was a powerhouse DJ. He could scratch, his production value and bag of DJ tricks were off the hook, and his music selections were as good as if I'd made them myself; Eric B. *loved* James Brown. Most important, he set up a rock-solid beat foundation for his rapper.

His rapper was Rakim. And Rakim *was* the best I ever heard.

Rakim brought so much new thought and technique to the game when he rhymed, it was like he singlehandedly reinvented the art form of being an MC. When it came to verbal acrobatics, no other MC came close. If everybody else's raps were like nursery rhymes, Rakim's were like Shakespeare.

Before Rakim, MCs would rhyme "cat" with "bat," or maybe "pretty" and "witty" if they wanted to get cute. Rakim rhymed polysyllabic words like "residence" and "presidents." Before Rakim, people started and ended verses in complete thoughts. Rakim would leave you hanging with an idea, just to make it rhyme, but finish the thought in the next sentence. Before Rakim, most rappers would set up one rhyme per line. Rakim would load up entire verses with so many continuous rhymes, I'd have to listen to them three or four times just to catch everything, marveling at how every phrase was a hook, every verse a complicated play on words.

Rakim was doing for rapping what I had done for DJing; he saw the limits of what was out there and figured he could do more. I could see him down in his own basement with a pen and a pad and a head so full of ideas, he couldn't write them all down fast enough.

Out West on the DJ front, Dr. Dre and DJ Quik showed that DJs were blowing up, and that they weren't just cutting records, they were cutting tracks too—DJs were elevating themselves and becoming record producers.

It took me back and got me thinking about the music in new ways, but I still didn't know how I was going to get back in the game. My contacts were gone. The old joints were closed. The block parties were long over. Where did that leave me and all my big ideas?

Downtown.

The Soho crowd had suddenly fallen in line with this new thing called hip hop. They wouldn't come uptown so I had to go down. Anywhere I played downtown, any club was always sold out.

At first I may have felt out of place playing these gigs. I may have felt a little weird in this strange setting. But I was also starting to feel like I was making people happy. I was getting 'em dancing. I was serving them by serving up the beats.

COWBOY'S LESSON (LOVE & DEATH)

It was the end of the eighties and I was slowly coming back. Playing whether I wanted to or not. Rocking little clubs downtown, uptown, crosstown, and out of town. Taking whatever gigs that came to me. Not being too proud to ask for the ones that didn't. Didn't matter whether it was teenagers or adults, black or white. I played.

Didn't matter if I missed my kids like crazy—I hadn't seen Tawanna, JoJo, and Lalonnie in a couple years 'cause Paulette One had moved without telling anybody where she was going. Didn't matter if I had family problems—Mom's health was failing and her mind was tormented. Didn't matter that my car was tore up or my place was run down. Despite the problems, my spirit was being restored, bit by bit and piece by piece.

Then one day in September of 1989, the phone rang.

"Flash, Cowboy's dead."

Three days later, I was in a South Bronx funeral home, wearing a black suit and standing over a casket, looking at my dead friend. Didn't matter that the guys were there and I hadn't talked to some of 'em in more than five years. Didn't care that there was way too much drama between us guys. For the moment, all that mattered was that one of my soldiers was gone.

The undertakers had done the best they could to make him up, but Keith was little more than skin and bones. This wasn't the Cowboy I remembered. The body lying in front of me wasn't the smiling, swaggering braggart who parted the crowd at 63 Park all those years ago, knocked a nigga out in order to get his hands on the mic, then rocked it all night long. It wasn't the body of the greatest MC to pump up a crowd I had ever seen. It was the body of a man who'd been ravaged by crack cocaine.

It could have been me. I loved the base just as much as Keith. When everything fell apart in '83, I'd heard Cowboy had hit the pipe hard. Even before that, when everybody else wanted cars and jewels instead of money in the bank, Cowboy spent his pay on cocaine.

Looking at my friend, the tears started to come. Didn't know why I was spared while he wasn't. Couldn't understand how somebody so full of life and love and talent and energy could be cut down by fame, fortune, and drugs.

I found myself asking God why he took Cowboy when my man had so much to give. He had a gift for effortlessly bringing good times to thousands of people. Why didn't he get a chance to get straight? Why did things get all fucked up for Grandmaster Flash and the Furious Five?

As I sat listening to Cowboy's eulogy, I felt a fire go out inside of me. I couldn't answer the questions I was asking. The Five were gone forever.

I went home that afternoon and felt more alone than ever. For some reason, I picked up the phone and called an old friend who had always been a great listener.

An hour later, I was over at Joanne's place, standing in her doorway with tears in my eyes. I was heartbroken, but being with Joanne felt like a weight lifting off my shoulders. And even though she had tears in her eyes too, I could also see peace in her soul, and that was something I didn't have.

"He was my first MC," I told her. "He was my baby."

"Now he's at peace," she reminded me.

"He had the most incredible voice ever," I lamented.

"And he could turn a crowd out till the breakadawn," Joanne chuckled.

"There's never gonna be another one like him," I wept.

"Thank God for that," she said again, smiling. "I don't think the Bronx could take it."

Even through my tears, I laughed. Another Cowboy would have been a handful.

We took a walk and ended up in Mott Haven Park. We sat and watched a pack of kids play twenty-one, half of them in Patrick Ewing jerseys and half wearing Air Jordans. Didn't look like they were having fun out there, not like me and Cowboy and the rest of the Five used to. These kids were throwing elbows and talking trash like they were out for blood, balling like it was serious business.

After a while, I finally spoke. "I feel like it's my fault."

"How's that?"

"Cowboy tried to get at me a year ago for some money," I continued. "I told him I couldn't do nothing for him 'cause I had no ends."

"So?"

"I didn't need the bother and it felt like he was dragging me down. But now I can't stop wondering if there was something I could have done."

"Flash," Joanne said, looking me in the eye, "do you really think you have that much power in the universe?"

The lump in my throat came back. Joanne continued: "It's normal to feel guilty, angry, lonely, and confused when somebody you love dies. And when it happens fast, sometimes there aren't any answers. But it's all normal . . . and it's all good, Flash."

How could what I was feeling be all good?

"Cowboy made his own decisions," said Joanne. "You make yours. And I make mine. We can all help each other, but we can't do anything for somebody who doesn't want to be helped, baby. Except love 'em. Did you love Cowboy?"

"Yeah," I said as I started to cry again.

"Then you did all you could."

"What am I s'posed to do now?"

"Just keep on loving him."

Found myself at home that night, asking the same old question . . . again.

Where do I go from here?

Except this time, that question was coming from deep in my soul, deeper than anything I'd ever felt before. This time, it wasn't about what was happening on the outside, it was about what was happening on the inside.

Somewhere in the back of my mind and the bottom of my heart, I had always believed that someday, somehow, I'd be a star again—that's why I was getting out there and hustling gigs. And somewhere in there, I'd also believed that the Furious Five would have something to do with it.

When Cowboy died, the bubble burst. I could keep going the way I was, playing my little gigs and doing my little thing, but now I was face-to-face with the same fear I had lying there on Penny's couch. I was thirty-two years old and it already felt like my best days were behind me.

Maybe my life was as good as it would ever get.

Maybe there was no comeback in my future.

Maybe I had to give up my hopes and dreams.

What would I replace them with?

Could I dream new dreams?

Could I be happy again?

I couldn't stop thinking like that. Couldn't turn my brain off. When I was still awake at two in the morning and I couldn't take it anymore, I called Joanne again.

"I'm going crazy!" I screamed.

"Then come over," she told me.

An hour later, I was drinking herbal tea over at Joanne's crib.

"All my life, I've been going somewhere," I said. "Always been headed toward something better."

"Who's to say you aren't headed toward something better now?" Joanne asked.

"How could that be? There's no party . . . there's no career . . . there's no action. I don't have shit going on! Nothing!"

I was worked up, but Joanne was calm.

"Was the action the thing that was making you happy?"

I wanted to blurt out yes, but didn't. Instead, I thought about the Sugar Hill days. That was supposed to be my brightest hour, but all I could remember was the lying, the betrayals, and the pain . . . the darkness. Sure, there were some good times, but they weren't going through my mind.

Maybe I wasn't really happy when I was flying high.

"No," I told Joanne. "The action wasn't it."

My confession sat there. And Joanne let it be.

In the silence, I thought about the kids on the basketball court yesterday afternoon. Wondered why they were playing in the first place. Didn't look like they were playing for fun, looked like they were trying out for the NBA.

What about me? Was I supposed to be having fun? Or was being a DJ supposed to be work? I couldn't dream of doing anything else with my life but playing music and keeping the beat. But going about it these days was not making me happy.

"Your life's been one crazy ride, Flash. Living in the fast lane like you did would have gotten anybody's heart pumping and nerves jumping like a four-alarm fire. Problem is, the alarm's still going off in your head, but there's no fire anymore. You need to turn off the noise, baby."

"That's crazy," I told Joanne. "Hasn't been any noise in my life in years. That's the *real* problem."

"Really? 'Cause you could still be out there getting high all you wanted . . . if that's what you really wanted. But you could also be dead like Cowboy."

She had me. I had to thank God again for my life, no matter what it looked like.

"You want to be happy again, right?"

"Yeah," I said.

"Not the get-high kind of happy, but real, lasting peace, right?"

"I want the kind of happiness you got," I told Joanne.

"Then it won't matter how you get there. Everything you want and everything you need you already have."

That rocked my world.

I wanted to argue. I wanted to tell her all the stuff I wanted and needed that I didn't have. But I didn't.

"What do I do?" I asked.

"This thing you're feeling, it's not like a heavy rock you can just put down when you get tired. All that stuff you used to do to keep the party going, you need to replace it with something."

"Something like what?"

"Something spiritual," she told me.

"You mean like God?"

"You can call it whatever you want," she continued, "but I call it love."

Love.

I had all kinds of love in my life, didn't I? I loved my sisters. I loved my kids. I loved my mom. I loved my pals Mike and Bee. I loved the girls in my life. I have to admit that I even loved Dad. I definitely loved the music and the beats. But what did all of those things have in common?

What did love mean?

The question haunted me. The great love of my life was Sweet Pea, Paulette Jeffrey. Even though I had messed up that relationship, that relationship never really went away. Paulette was my sure-enough soul mate. We tried, but could never quite stay away from each other. At the same time, we could never quite get it together.

I loved Sweet Pea, she loved me, and yet that love never went anywhere. That love never made us happy.

"Flash, when was the last time you were truly happy?" asked Joanne, whose wholesome friendship helped keep me healthy.

It took me a second to think about that. It certainly wasn't the long nights at the Hilltop or the dope spot. It wasn't playing for huge crowds of people all over the world. It wasn't all the girls and the sex and the drugs and the booze and the private planes and shopping sprees and cars or any of that stuff.

"It was that night at the Audubon."

"Oh yeah?" she asked. "Why then?"

Had to think about it for a minute. Sure, we were the kings of New York that night. And I wasn't about to lie that I didn't love hearing everybody screaming my name. But still, I had a feeling that wasn't what Joanne was hinting at. So I closed my eyes and remembered back to that golden moment between me and the crowd:

Grandmaster!

       Zuka-Zuka

Cut faster!

       Zuka-Zuka

Grandmaster!

       Zuka-Zuka

Cut faster!

ZUKA-*Zuka*

Everybody was keeping the beat. The crowd wasn't there to stroke my ego and I wasn't there to hear them scream my name. It was about the energy between us. I was giving it to them and they were giving it back. Each time it passed back and forth, it got more powerful.

It was that euphoric union.

The beat was love.

Love was the beat.

It wasn't mine.

It wasn't theirs.

It belonged to all of us.

The only way to keep it alive was to give it away.

"You've got a beautiful spirit and a curious mind," Joanne told me. "You've got so much to give. If you can give it away, Flash, you can be happy again. That's what love is."

LIGHT

Joanne's words stuck with me.

My old notions about who I thought I was and what I thought I needed to be happy had to go away. The problem was, I couldn't forget them.

What, then, was I supposed to do?

Joanne gave me a book. It had a lot of deep ideas, but one that jumped out at me was that it was impossible to dismiss a thought directly. Instead, it had to be replaced with a new one. I could put down a heavy load I was carrying in the physical realm, but on a mental, emotional, and spiritual plane, that book said I couldn't stop thinking a destructive thing without replacing the idea.

Couldn't stop regretting the past without having hope for the future.

Couldn't stop being angry without taking a chance on forgiveness.

Is that what my new thoughts were supposed to be?

"Don't worry," Joanne reassured me. "The answers will all come in time. Just read this book next."

The next book was all about Eastern philosophy. I couldn't relate at first but I began to read and slowly started to notice the similarities between Eastern and Western philosophies that the first book discussed. Both talked about one God. Both said the same thing that Joanne did—that God is love. Both talked about forgiveness as being the key to salvation; if you can forgive your enemies, you can forgive yourself. Both said that true happiness came from things like peace, acceptance, love, and service.

"Keep looking for the similarities rather than the differences," Joanne said.

Both books also said that by forgetting about the self, one finds peace.

I devoured those two books and everything else I could get my hands on. Felt good just doing something about the way I felt. But how was I supposed to forget who I was in order to find myself?

"Just keep on doing what you're doing," Joanne told me when I asked her that. "It'll all work itself out."

"When?" I asked.

"When the time is right," she smiled. "You're on a spiritual path, Flash. All you have is this moment right now."

Spiritual path or otherwise, I hated waiting. I could wrap my head around the idea that it took time to change, but not my heart. And as for the concept of this moment right now being the most important one in my life? All I knew about the here and now back then was that I was miserable.

I still felt like I was nobody, and that was a dark thought.

"Just keep doing what you're doing, Flash. Just keep moving toward the light," Joanne said.

Move toward the light.

It sounded great, but was no substitute for my thoughts.

I still had anger and resentment for the people from my past.

I still had fear about the future.

And I still wasn't happy about where I was in the now.

Later I would read a book called *The Power of Now,* which would put all these ideas into perspective, but back in the early nineties, it was still difficult for me to understand.

These new ideas, though, weren't completely new. Within them, I recognized something from my past. I flashed back to my childhood, the synagogue, the Kingdom Hall, the nights when Mommy prayed to her savior. None of those concepts stuck with me for very long. Yet that spiritual stuff obviously meant something to my family; it helped them through. I needed something to help me through.

Meanwhile, I didn't feel any better about the gigs I had—the private parties, the little clubs, and the drug dealer tapes. Moving toward the light didn't put more money in my pocket to pay for the things my kids needed, and it didn't help that I couldn't get in touch with three of them. But what had I done about that?

"Have you thought about looking for Paulette and them?" That was Jean, my son Kareem's mother. I'd been seeing Kareem and her on the regular, trying to make up for lost time.

To be honest, I hadn't thought about it that way. Initially, I'd been so pissed off that Paulette Dawson had the nerve to disappear like she did (even though I wasn't the best father), I actually thought I was punishing her by not doing something about it. But after talking to Jean and Joanne, it seemed like I was drinking poison but hoping Paulette would get sick. In the end, it was my kids I stood to hurt the most and they hadn't done anything wrong.

Even Mom was clearheaded enough to tell me straight one time when I went to visit at her little one-room apartment: "Butsy, you listen to your mama. You need to be a father to those kids."

"Maybe you and Kareem could go looking for 'em," Jean said. So a few days a week, Kareem and I would jump in my old hooptie ride—the BMW was long gone by then—and go searching.

Maybe looking for the rest of my kids would make me feel better.

While I drove, Kareem talked, and I learned that Kareem was interested in how things worked. Turned out he was more into plumbing and elbow joints and pipes than he was into turntables and music, but I couldn't help but see the similarities between my son and me.

He wasn't more than thirteen—where had he learned this stuff?

When I asked, Kareem shrugged. Just like I did when Pete Jones asked me the same thing.

Maybe Penny was right.

Maybe what we do is inborn.

Kareem and I would be out knocking on doors and asking at every corner whether anyone knew the whereabouts of my kids. Some days were straight-up frustrating. But along the way, I got to know my son Kareem, who later became an incredible plumber. And even when we'd come home empty-handed, I was truly grateful for our time together.

Then I found out I was about to be a father again, thanks to a beautiful woman named Pam. Thanks to my time with Kareem, I vowed to be there for my bright young son Keith from the day he was born.

Despite Paulette Dawson's efforts, I eventually found her and the kids. She still did everything she could to keep me away, and I didn't have the heart to fight her to the mat. But once again, the God of love stepped in.

Lalonnie—Paulette's and my youngest—was fifteen by now, and would cut her last class to come see me so that her mom wouldn't know about it. One day after a few months, she sat me down and said, "Dad, I've always heard Mom's side of the story. Now I want to hear yours."

I knew I had to tell her the truth if I wanted my daughter in my life. So I told her everything—the good, the bad . . . all of it.

I'd never felt so small in front of a child. I was ashamed, remembering a lot of the things I'd done, but the truth set me free. Lalonnie went home and told Paulette Dawson she wanted to be in my life. Paulette was still mad, and rightfully so. I'd been an asshole. But the power of love won out. Lalonnie kept at our relationship, so did I, and we became extremely close. In time, the same thing happened with JoJo and Tawanna.

Thank God.

There was another thing I could wrap my heart around—a new golden age of hip hop. As the early nineties took shape, rap music got even better. Not only better, but more diverse.

There was Long Island's finest, EPMD. They had become the underground kings and had earned the utmost respect when they made a point of doing things their way, refusing to cater to radio-friendly hooks and imaging. Also shunning the commercial tip was Kool G Rap, who could get just as deep and complicated with his lyrics as Rakim, but with a gangster's edge. Big Daddy Kane was the smooth operator, the mack on wax, the Iceberg Slim of rap. Salt-N-Pepa, MC Lyte, and Queen Latifah released red-hot jams to establish the female voice of rap once and for all. The diabolical Biz Markie established himself as the class clown. And Slick Rick, with his laid-back style and uncanny storytelling, oozed charisma from his every pore.

Gang Starr stayed true to the old-school formula of equal billing for both the rapper and the DJ, while upping the level of their game; Guru had first-rate social rhymes and technical sophistication while DJ Premier's ability to cut left me speechless every time I heard him in action. Same thing went for Pete Rock, who had insane musical talent. In fact, both those guys were full-fledged producers, following in the footsteps of Marley Marl and his 808 sound whose big low tom *BOOM* started rap's love affair with the thumping bass.

Then there was the Native Tongue family—Jungle Brothers, A Tribe Called Quest, and De La Soul. The progeny of Afrika Bambaataa's Zulu Nation, they were bringing a whole new style to the art form, mixing all kinds of musical influences only Bam had thought to use back in the seventies: jazz, house, techno, classic rock, blues, folk, and even country made for new sampling styles. Every time I heard a new cut from one of these cats, I got new ideas of my own. Their raps ranged from Afrocentric and abstract thought to off-the-wall, outright gibberish that was both brain and tongue twisting. Whatever it was, you needed a college education and a thesaurus to get all the references and jokes. It was unbelievably creative and poetic. And with future Native Tongue family members like Black Sheep and Leaders of the New School making tapes from the underground, the future of hip hop looked brighter than ever.

Maybe the block party was gone, but the scene was exploding and my fever for the beats was hotter than it had ever been. I found a way to work the music into my sets, regardless of the venue. And every now and then, a bright-eyed kid would come up to the turntables and ask, "Who the hell was that you was rockin'?"

Anytime I saw one of those faces and got to spread the gospel of hip hop, I felt the love, the light, and the spirit entering back into my soul.

"They want you."

That was my booking agent. She knew everybody back in the day.

"I've been agenting artists," she told me when I asked her what she'd been up to. She'd been working with guys like FAB 5 FREDDY and Bam and the Rock Steady Crew. After I told her about what I had cooking, she smiled and said, "I can get you more work. And better gigs."

She and my new attorney, Roberta Korus, put their money where their mouth was and made it rain. The gigs were small at first, but my booking agent never stopped hustling, and what started as a drizzle became a steady flow.

Unlike the Queen, my booking agent was up-front with me, her accounting was professional, and everything we did was laid out on the table. "What's good for you is good for both of us," she said, "and if you deal straight with me, I'll deal straight right back at you."

As the gigs got better, so did the money. Most important of all, she made sure that I got paid, and when promoters came at me to do deals on the outside, I told them they needed to go through my agent.

"C'mon, Flash!" promoters would beg sometimes when I was on the road by myself. "These people wanna hear you! What do I have to do to get you to play again tomorrow night, you know, under the table?"

After all I'd been through, shady business deals didn't feel right. Didn't feel like moving toward the light.

"You want me, talk to my agent."

I took care of her and she took care of me. Business was improving. I was finally able to get a good night's sleep without being tortured by regret.

But where did I fit in? Was it my destiny to be a club DJ whose best days were behind him? That question still lingered in my mind after my head hit the pillow. The answer would always come back to the things I was learning along my spiritual path.

The light is where you find the love.
Love is the key to happiness.
Happiness is the by-product of being of service.

But I was about to learn that happiness and service sometimes come in strange ways.

YOU CHOOSE YOUR PARENTS

It sounded like complete bullshit to me.

The book I was reading said that everybody chooses their own parents. It said that every unconscious soul knows what it needs in order to flourish in the next life, therefore the soul selects two people in the world most perfectly suited to be its parents in the moment before its physical conception.

I was devouring every spiritual book I could get my hands on, and while I understood most of what I read, I couldn't get my mind around this new idea to save my life. When I thought about my folks, I have to admit, I didn't believe it could be true.

I thought of how Dad had beaten my ass and the mental and physical anguish Mom had to endure. Maybe I didn't see a lot of traditional families growing up in the South Bronx, but nobody I knew saw their dad bust up their mom with a frying pan. Nobody I knew saw the police take their mom away in a straitjacket. And the more I thought about the idea that my spirit could have chosen my parents, the more I felt the hole in my soul start to open up again.

Made me wonder what good ever came from such a fucked-up situation. Made me think about my own life as a parent. Made me think about how little I knew about showing up for my own kids. Was that a good thing? I might not have been available, but at least I didn't beat them.

Would I have beaten them if I had been around? Would I have beaten them if I'd been as frustrated as my dad?

I had a ton of questions but no answers.

Then the phone rang again.

Summer 1994.

Penny was on the other end of the line. She was crying, barely able to speak.

"Everything seemed fine when I saw Mom yesterday, but then it got really hot . . . and you know how she was about opening the windows . . . and then she couldn't get her air . . ." Then her voice broke off.

"Penny? Are you there?"

Silence.

"Penny," I said, "what happened? What happened to Mommy?"

"She's—"

More silence.

"Flash, Mommy's gone."

I felt sick.

No good-bye. No questions answered. My mother was dead. Sent me back into the hole in my soul. Back into the darkness.

I felt guilty.

What kind of son lets his mother die alone in a hot apartment?

Despite my shame, I also felt a bit relieved.

No matter how much I tried to tell myself I was glad my mother was at peace, I was relieved I didn't have to worry about her anymore.

I laid awake at night with my thoughts running though my mind.

Once again, I called Joanne.

Once again, she invited me over and made me tea.

"It's hard to see the people we love pass on," she said.

"You don't understand," I told Joanne. "She shouldn't have been alone."

"Maybe it was her time," Joanne said.

How the hell could it have been my mother's time? And what kind of God or love or whatever would let her suffocate to death in a hot little apartment?

"If her work in this life was done," Joanne said, as I struggled to keep my opinions to myself, "then it was time for her to move on. And maybe her spirit knew that."

Without saying good-bye? Without finding some mental peace? I couldn't stop the questions even if I'd tried.

"I don't think you understand," I told Joanne. "My mother wasn't right in her mind or her spirit for most of her life. And if she didn't know much in this life, then her spirit sure didn't either."

"She knew to believe in you. She saw you had mechanical talent. She put you in vocational school. She got you where you needed to go in life . . . and raised four other kids without any help. If that isn't spirit, then tell me what is."

Yet again, Joanne said exactly what I needed to hear.

I had always loved my mother, but it had been a very long time since I'd thought about how strong she'd been for her children.

"You can honor her by remembering what she did right by you."

I remembered: She had been responsible for my formal education when it came to electronics and things that I knew about sound equipment. She had known to do it because she'd had mechanical gifts of her own—my mother was an ingenious seamstress. Mom knew how to build things. She also knew how to use the tools available to her and I saw her work miracles with her sewing machine.

Maybe the idea that my spirit was nurtured by hers wasn't so crazy after all.

If I still had any doubts about it, though, what happened next removed them all.

"Butsy, it's Violet."

I hadn't heard from my oldest sister in a long time. It was about nine months after Mom had passed and the family had tried to keep closer, but Violet lived in Brooklyn and might as well have been on the dark side of the moon.

"Dad's sick."

This time, my feelings were a lot more subdued. I didn't feel the same things for Dad that I had felt for Mom. I didn't care about my mother and my father in the same way. And if the truth were to be known, I was still angry. After Mom had died, Penny had gone to tell him about it and came back to the Bronx with steam pouring out her ears.

"You know what that motherfucker had to say when I told him she had passed?" Penny exclaimed, her face beet red. "He actually had the nerve to utter the words, 'Another one bites the dust.' Can you believe that?"

I didn't want to believe it, but I did. That was our dad.

Far as I was concerned, I didn't need any more drama in my life and if he was sick, maybe it was best to just let him be. But I also knew that if I didn't go to him, it would only make the hole in my soul that much worse.

So I swallowed my feelings and went to see my father.

Early 1995.

It had been years since I'd seen my dad in person. Even if he hadn't been sick, Dad looked small. I might have been confused about a lot of things regarding my dad, but he was reduced and no longer scary. The boxer was losing his last fight.

At first, I just sat with him. We'd talk a little—he'd ask me this and that and make idle conversation—but I'd keep my feelings to myself. It always felt like there was something more he wanted to say. So I kept going back to visit him, and like Joanne had done with me, I listened and I waited.

Eventually, Dad spoke.

"Over there," Dad said, pointing a finger at an old cabinet. "Open it up and tell me what you find."

When I looked, I found dozens of fliers from shows I'd played in the seventies. One said:

Black Door Productions Presents:

EASTER WEEK-END

with

"GRANDMASTER FLASH"

Disco Bee—3 M.C.'s

KEITH-KEITH, MELLE MEL & KID CREOLE

Dad had saved them all.

"I watched you. I followed your career and kept track of the things you did."

"How?" I asked, as a lump built in my throat.

"I got the word. Sometimes people would tell me. First I started collecting all those fliers ... then the records ... then newspaper clippings. 'Course I seen you on TV. And when that movie came out"—Dad smiled, talking about *Wild Style*—"we all went to see it. That was something."

This was something.

"Even though I didn't come see you play, I knew what you was doing."

Hearing Dad say that filled the hole in my soul. Whatever it was I'd been keeping out of my heart all these years moved back where it belonged and fell into place.

Then he said words I'd been wanting to hear all my life.

"I was proud of you."

That's when it hit me: maybe my spirit had always seen what my eyes or even my heart couldn't. Maybe Dad—despite everything—*was* destined to be my father. I could have been unforgiving about how he beat me and kept his records away from me. But by the grace of God, I went left instead of right at that road. Instead of hating the music and hating the beat, I figured, *Dag, this must be some special stuff for him to keep beating my ass like that.* And instead of driving me away, it compelled me toward records and turntables. It drew me to the music.

It moved me toward the light.

I could have been hard-hearted about how he left us. Could have given up on my dreams at any point along the way, but Dad was a fighter and so was I. By not helping me with what I needed to do for myself, Dad helped me become the man I was.

Like Mom had been able to pass on her gift of mechanics, Dad gave me his love of music and his fighting spirit.

Over the next month, I sat with my father and talked about the thing we both loved more than anything—music. At the time, jazz was big in hip hop. A Tribe Called Quest had made it their thing. Guru from Gang Starr took jazz and laid it down live, recording several solo albums with jazz greats like Donald Byrd, Roy Ayers, and Lonnie Liston Smith. Since

I didn't know anybody who knew more about jazz than Dad, I got an idea.

I pulled out his turntable that I was never allowed to touch. He wasn't going to bang my hand this time. He wasn't gonna slap me or nothing. It finally was my turn to shine for my dad.

"Dad, I'm doing this thing called producing. In producing, there's this thing called sampling. Sampling is where I break the elements of a song down to their smallest parts. I'm trying to capture solos: drums, bass, guitars . . . hell, if you know of some hot piccolo shit, let me hear it."

Dad shuffled to his shelves and thumbed through his massive library of records. Then came back with a mischievous smile and an armload of LPs.

"You mean like this?" he'd say, every time he came back.

For the last few months of his life, "You mean like this" became my dad's mantra. It became his gift to me. If I asked for specifics—say, a hot drum solo—Dad always knew where to look. Without missing a beat, my father came back with shaking hands and put on the most amazing bits of sound I could imagine—things I'd never heard another DJ play. Things I could chop up and break down until jazz, funk, soul, and rhythm and blues all became hip hop.

We'd sit for hours. We'd dig through the stacks finding gem after gem, to the point where I could only hope to remember where these beautiful breaks were hidden. This time, when I would lay my hands on his records, he smiled. "Whatever happens, son, I want you to have my records."

When my father finally passed, I didn't feel the same sense of regret that I felt with Mom. All I had was a sense of beautiful gratitude for the time I had recently spent with him.

All that was left was love.

BACK TO THE ONE

As the light got brighter, my life continued to move forward.

Everything headed in a positive direction. Work was good, I was even traveling out of town to play; people were starting to request me by name again. I was striving to be a better, more present dad with Tawanna, JoJo, Lalonnie, Kareem, and baby Keith.

Everything those books had said was true. The light and the happiness I felt were the by-product of the choices I made. Taking the kids to school. Buying toys and clothes. Throwing birthday parties. The more I was of service to my family and the people around me, the more I felt the power of love building inside.

That didn't mean I wasn't still confused about a lot of things, especially when it came to getting mine professionally. It was the mid-nineties by now and I was watching hip hop give birth to yet another age: the age of achievement. Guys like Sean "Puffy" Combs and the Wu-Tang Clan were controlling their own business interests in ways artists hadn't ever thought to do. What Russell Simmons had started, they were taking to whole new levels of getting paid.

Puffy had his own record label, Bad Boy Entertainment, and was negotiating big-money product endorsements and building a stable of red-hot artists, just like Russell had. But unlike Russell, Puffy hitched his name to the Bad Boy talent pool. He put himself in the public eye, built his name up, and created a new personality profile in rap music: the hip hop mogul.

As for the Wu-Tang Clan, they grew a fan base by establishing a franchise and brand name, then released hit after hit, each one selling more than the last. The Wu-Tang business model and work ethic earned those cats more money than rappers in my day had ever seen. To top it all off, they *really* began thinking outside the box when they attached their name to a clothing line called Wu-Wear.

For a minute, I veered back into my old thoughts, the ones I had before I'd begun moving toward the light. Once again I asked the questions: Was I a sucker for going out like I did with Sugar Hill? Was I a chump for not standing the test of time in the rap game? Had I forgotten who I was and where I fit in?

"Don't listen to the voices in your head, Flash," said Joanne. "Just keep doing what you love."

What I loved was the art form of the DJ, and that form was moving forward in ways I couldn't imagine. DJs were doing things that blew my mind: DJ Qbert's ability to create new techniques made the turntable art form sound like some kind of strange language. DJ Shadow and Cut Chemist were deconstructing records down to such small components—with beats and breaks I couldn't identify in the first place—that it hardly sounded like turntablism at all. Even if the DJ wasn't getting rich like the MC, these guys made the art form sound like being in a real band. Most important, these guys were in the game for the same reason that I had been: the love of it.

It still meant something to be a DJ.

But what, then, did it mean to be DJ Grandmaster Flash?

Tuesday nights in late 1996, I spun records and broadcasted live from WBLS at Bentley's, one of the top spots in Manhattan, thanks to the advice of DJs like Marly Mar and Red Alert and Chuck Chill-Out, who had figured out how to parlay their celebrity onto the radio. Now our science was something we could do across the airwaves.

Just like in the old days at the Fever, people came to Bentley's to be seen. But unlike the old days, they weren't there to see me, and I'd be lying if I said that didn't sting a little.

One night, the door to the DJ booth swung open and a hulking dark-skinned figure came in and set his heavy frame in a chair.

When I looked up, I saw who it was—Biggie Smalls.

By then, Biggie was the hottest MC anywhere. Any time I put on one of his cuts, the whole club would go bonkers and so would I—he had incredible flows and fantastic freestyles, and I saw the same thing in him that I had seen in the original Furious Five MCs—this amazing presence that made him a bona fide superstar.

My first thought was to give him a shout-out and put a mic in his hand. But just as I had that thought he said, "Flash, please don't mention me."

If I had, the place would have gone totally apeshit and he'd have been mobbed.

"I just wanna sit here and chill for a minute."

I kept quiet long enough for him to take a load off, then kept quiet and listened while he talked about his concerns about his new album.

As he got up to leave, he gave me a pound, and though he didn't have to, Biggie let me know that he appreciated my work.

"Wouldn't be none of this if you and them hadn't gone before."

Hearing him say that was like the first time I heard "Freedom" on the radio. Felt like when I laid my eyes on that graffiti piece in Europe on our first tour . . . or holding Tawanna, JoJo, Lalonnie, or Keith for the first time . . . or driving around the Bronx with Kareem, realizing my kid was just like me.

It was one of those moments when it hits you: the world is a lot bigger than you think it is.

That's how I got my answer.

That's what it meant to be Grandmaster Flash.

I am one of the best to ever do it.

But undisputedly I am the first.

And nothing was going to change that.

First is forever.

Right around that time, I was DJing a movie premiere when I ran into a writer friend of mine, Nelson George.

"Flash, there's this guy by the name of Chris Rock. He's a comedian."

"Yeah," I said. "*Saturday Night Live.*"

"He wants to talk to you."

"What for?"

"He's doing a weekly series for HBO next season," Nelson said. "He wants you to be his DJ."

"What, like on TV?"

"Yeah."

"*National* TV?"

"Yes, national TV." Nelson laughed. "Can I give him your number?"

I didn't believe Nelson. Chris Rock was going to call me to DJ on national television? So I gave him my lawyer's number instead to see if it was real.

A month later the phone rang.

It was my lawyer telling me that Chris Rock had a contract for me.

The contract talked about how this was going to be a real job. With real pay. The contract talked about limos picking me up. It talked about clothing endorsements and product placement.

A month after that, I was in my own dressing room at the Trevor Berbeck Theater in Manhattan, about to tape our first show. The producers had built me a platform and rigged the theater with a killer sound system they let me help design. I was thinking, *Dag, Chris could have picked from so many DJs. Why'd he pick me?*

"Because I always wanted to be a DJ," he told me right before we went on, "and you were always the baddest cat around."

Again, I couldn't put what I felt into words.

For the next four years, I was the *Chris Rock Show* DJ. For the next four years, I had an audience across America every Friday night.

Huge.

But bigger than hearing Chris say, "Ladies and Gentlemen, Grandmaster Flash," every week, I was reaching the biggest audience I ever had. I was reaching people in ways I never thought a DJ would.

Since then, the light has continued to shine. By the time *The Chris Rock Show* ended, my booking agent's phone was ringing off the hook. Thanks to her, Roberta, and Penny, I surrounded myself with a competent business team who started marketing the name Grandmaster Flash.

I'd be in a club in Tokyo one night, Munich the next, and a week later

I was playing the closing ceremonies at the Commonwealth Games in England in front of 40,000 people, including the Queen. Yes, the Queen of England.

I played the MTV Video Music Awards. I started hosting a weekly show on Sirius Satellite Radio. I signed equipment endorsements for needles, mixers, and turntables. I finally released an album of my own, called *The Adventures of Grandmaster Flash on the Wheels of Steel*. I had another beautiful little girl, Christina, with a beautiful woman named Angelique. I bought a house—after all the years of bumping around, crashing on couches, renting apartments, and never having a place to call my own, I finally owned property. I finally had a place for my family to call home.

Then the awards started coming in. It started with donating artifacts to the Experience Music Project in Seattle. Then it was the Bronx Walk of Fame. Then it was the key to the city of Cleveland. There were many other prestigious awards, but I've never been more proud of anything I've received than when I was given the BET Icon Award. It was like the black entertainment community was saying, "You did something, something that made a difference in the world. Something that mattered." I was proud to hear my own people acknowledge, "You are a part of history now."

"It's time to write a book." One day, Mark Green, one of my closest advisers and a cat with a knack for thinking outside the box, came to me and said that. Mark made it happen.

Just after Christmas 2006, the phone rang.

"Flash, you heard the news?" It was Disco Bee. "James Brown died." I'd been out of town and barely even knew what time it was. But the news was a major wake-up call. Lately I'd been thinking about all the good things that were coming my way. I had an attitude that I was finally getting the props I deserved. When I heard about James Brown, it put me in my place.

More than anybody else, James Brown knew funk. James Brown knew beats. James Brown had been a guiding musical light, and I owed him respect. I was always very clear about something: no James Brown, no hip hop, no me. The best thing to do was to jump in my car and drive down to Harlem.

December 28, 2006. The Apollo Theater. His memorial service had the streets shut down for blocks.

"My name is Grandmaster Flash," I told one of the NYPD officers manning the barricade, "and I'm here to pay my respects to Mister James Brown."

Ten minutes later, I was sitting next to the Reverend Al Sharpton, gazing down at the casket that held the body of JB. I wasn't sad. I wasn't surprised. Just couldn't believe it.

"We're all humans," I told Reverend Sharpton, "and I know that we're all going to die. But I never actually thought that JB would ever be gone."

I sat there for the rest of the day, just lost in my thoughts. JB wasn't just *the* Godfather, he was *my* Godfather. God had spoken to me through his music—the maddening basslines and impossibly revolutionary rhythms. God had shown me how to pick the individual bits and pieces of instrumentation apart, thanks to James Brown's songs. My own father wasn't always around. But James Brown was.

In early 2007, Grandmaster Flash and the Furious Five were inducted into the Rock and Roll Hall of Fame. Receiving the award from Jay-Z was an honor in itself. Performing live on stage with Mel, Creole, Scorp, and Rahiem for the first time in years was an unbelievable thrill but I still missed Cowboy. Having my big sister Penny sit next to me at the awards ceremony was a gift. Being the first hip hop artists inducted was a reminder once again that we were there when it all started. As we do our thing, it hits me: after all the fights, the drama, and the tough times, I still love the guys with all my heart.

But still, what did it mean? Was my life's greatest accomplishment something to be visited in the past? Did it matter whether I'd be remembered when I was dead, or was it still important for me to reach as many people as I could?

If yes, where did I go now?

NOW

It's been a little more than a year since the Rock and Roll Hall of Fame. Now life's moving at the speed of light.

Now I'm a producer. Now I'm the international spokesperson for Trakktor Scratch software—bringing my techniques into the twenty-first century. Now I got an album in the works—*The Bridge* is coming out on the Adrenalin City Entertainment label. Now I got my own studio setup to record so I don't have to leave the house at three in the morning when my ideas come to me.

I've been playing out of town since the night of the awards ceremony. Didn't even have time to go home. Flew that night from New York to Singapore. Played a show. Flew from Singapore to Melbourne to Shanghai to Brussels to Barcelona to London to Miami to Houston to Las Vegas. Rocked the crowd every night and slept like a baby every day.

Now I'm home.

First time in a month.

I'm exhausted.

I want to sleep but I can't.

Partly it's the jet lag—my body doesn't know where it's at or what time it is, even if the clock on the wall says 5:45 A.M.

Partly it's because of all the things I have to do: Christina's mom keeps telling me we have a PTA meeting later on today. I need to go food shopping. I need to catch up on new jams. I need to get an electrician to finish the wiring in the new studio setup. Gotta go through the mail.

Partly it's because of the ideas percolating in my mind: I want to get back to the lab and the new projects I've been thinking about. Even thirty-five years into the game, there are still new styles to create and new horizons to cross. It's gonna be the best thing I've created yet.

New beats to find.

New ways to make you move.

New science to bring the music to the people.

Can't stop, won't stop, in my head or in my heart.

I head down into my studio. It's still dark. I'm a little out of sorts, but I can't believe how far I am from where I started. I have a yard. There's dew on the grass. Can't believe I have a lawn. It's late April and the air is already starting to lose its chill.

My day starts and I handle my business: the food shopping, the responsible dad stuff; I pay the bills and even find time to mow the lawn.

Toward the end of the day, my booking agent calls. "Flash, you know you got a gig tonight at Water Taxi Beach."

Damn. Forgot to check the schedule. Still a little road tired. But DJing parties is what I do.

Four hours later, I'm right where I'm supposed to be: with my two hands on the turntables. My partner DJ Demo set us up and got the crowd moving with his opening set.

By now, I'm almost an hour into my show. I'm about to make the transition between an uptempo remix of a hot Jay-Z jam and one of the move-your-ass jams off Kanye West's new album. Both songs are hot and I'm just as into the music as the crowd.

I hear the voices of some of my old friends from the old days: *The music these days doesn't have the same juice it did back when we was kids. The music these days ain't keeping it real.*

"Keeping it real?" I ask when somebody says that. "What's real to me and you might not be real to someone else. You might not be into Jay-Z and Kanye but that doesn't make 'em any less real than the party jams we used to rock."

I don't judge. Sean Kingston gets me going just as much as "Good Times" or "Apache." The only person I need to keep it real for is right here in front of me. You. Right there in the crowd.

Right now in this moment, there is no old school. There is no new school. There's only the now school.

Now is all we have.

I like to visit the past, but I don't want to live there.

That means looking for new jams to keep the party real.

FLASH'S UNIVERSAL DJ RULE NUMBER FIVE:
A DJ is always listening for what's next.

I watch the ripple effect as the crowd recognizes the Kanye jam and hollers their approval. As they point and smile and shout at the DJ booth—*That's my song, Flash!*—my head bobs a little harder. I'm giving them this good time, they're giving it right back to me, and I'm giving it right back to them.

That's my job.

That's my responsibility to the crowd.

I'm what I've always been: a servant.

Suddenly it hits me; my life has always been leading up to one thing: this moment. Now this one. And now this one . . . and now this one.

The good parts: the beats, the parties, the techniques, my children, my family, and the love and continuation of a spiritual guiding light in my life.

The bad parts: shady business deals, foolish decisions, drug addiction, broken homes, and broken hearts.

The lessons and the blessings. The Queen. Miss Rose. Ray Chandler. Pete Jones. Herc. Bam. Mel, Cowboy, and the rest of the guys. Mike and Bee. Penny and Lilly. Carmetta and Violet. Tawanna, Joe, Lalonnie, Kareem, Keith, and Christina.

Mommy.

Dad.

It's all good. It's all right. It's all necessary. All of it has been necessary to tell my story. Everything is everything.

I close my eyes. The music plays and the crowd grooves on.

Acknowledgments

Grandmaster Flash acknowledges:

BIG THANKS to . . .

Sal Abbatiello, for allowing me to bring hip hop into your club Disco Fever when no one else wanted it. Morton Berger, R.I.P. Thanks to you and Judge Brient I was able to get back my name. I didn't get any financial reparation, but I gained the freedom to be me, Joseph Saddler, a.k.a. Grandmaster Flash.

My wonderful staff at Grandmaster Flash Enterprises: My faithful DJ partner, Percival Neptune, a.k.a. DJ Demo—thanks for never letting me down; Shelina Parker, my personal assistant—you kept your promise, thank you; I have money saved now. Rosemary Tully, my trusty attorney—your detailing drives me crazy, but thank you for protecting me. Antoine Joyce, a.k.a. Twizzle, for techinical production. Angela Thomas for PR.

Mark Green—thank you for your patience and the groundbreaking words that prompted me to do this book. Thanks to Roberta Korus, my first attorney.

To my friends from the Greer School: Carl and Carletta Epps; Clyde and Clifton Hollingsworth, Malcolm Giles, Clarence Williams, Sybil Greene. Foster care wasn't so bad because I had you guys as friends.

My best friends forever and DJ partners: E-Z Mike and Disco Bee. Kev Dog—I miss you and I love you dearly; you were a great friend. Monkey George—it may be that the Lord took you too soon, but God is love and I miss you. My best childhood friends in the whole world: Calvin Jackson, Gordon Upshaw, and Octavius Glenn. Joe Kidd—on that cold January morning, your words and the title "Grand Master" changed my life. Kool DJ AJ—thanks for being such a reliable opening DJ everywhere I played, especially that scary first night I played the Audubon Ballroom with the Furious Five. Casanova Crew and the Boston Road Crew—thanks for being the best security in my early years. I love you all.

Thanks to the good folks at Sirius: Geronimo, Steven B, Vanessa, Tanya, Neel, and the rest of the gang who make it happen.

Thanks to Pablo and everyone at Native Instruments. The only reason I went digital is because of Traktor Scratch, the best DJ application on the planet.

Thanks to Talib Kweli and his people.

Bill Adler—thanks for sharing your archives with us.

Geoff Martin—thank you for your patience; you asked so many damn questions, but I get it now. David Ritz—when I was told I was going to be interviewed by a guy on an issue so delicate, I said no, but you had an incredible and whimsical way of extracting information to create masterpieces. Janet Hill Talbert—for someone who is so soft-spoken, you are the ultimate of power without emanating it. Thanks also to Christian Nwachukwu, Tommy Semosh, Anne Watters, David Drake, Catherine Pollock, Mark Birkey, Frieda Duggan, Michael Collica, Kim Cacho, Rebecca Holland, Kate Duffy, Ed Crane, Vimi Santokhi, Rebecca Gardner, Rachel Horowitz, Louise Quayle, Stephen Rubin, Bill Thomas, Michael Palgon, the sales reps, and everyone else at the Doubleday Publishing Group.

Thanks to BET and Stephen Hill for the BET Icon Award. Thank you to all of the incredible people at the Rock and Roll Hall of Fame for making me the first DJ to receive such a prestigious honor. And thanks to some of the people I've admired throughout the years who finished what they started . . . and are still doing it: Russell Simmons, Mary J. Blige, Nelson George, Chris Rock, Leor Cohen, Kevin Lyles, Clive Davis, Quincy Jones, Jason Strauss, Noah Teppenburg, Oprah Winfrey, Maya Angelou, Ruby Dee, Steve Jobs, James Earl Jones, Dave Sirilnick, Bill and Melinda Gates, Warren Buffett, Mike Maulding, Sean Combs, Chris Lighty, Alan Heyman, Afrika Bambaataa, Michael Jordan, Magic Johnson, and Spike Lee.

Thanks to my granddaughters, Jakaya, Sashi, and Brynia. My grandsons, Lil Joe Joe and Bishme. My nieces Venescha, Kaleema, and Moma. My nephews, Poppy (R.I.P.), Dunnie, Ramel Kendall, Curtis and Darren (R.I.P.). Denise Howell, Pamela Howell (We got Keith, I promise.), Jean Sanders (Kareem's mother), Paulette Dawson, Angelique Jester (Christina's mom)—Thank you for my wonderful children, Nina Howell, Cherie Howell, Raquel Huston, Danielle Howell, Tay Tay, Precious, Christian, Niquye, William (Swann) Batton.

Paulette Jeffrey and Regina "Penny" Saddler—I was surely headed for the cemetery. Thank you for instilling in me that my time on earth wasn't done.

Ebony Howard, thank you for your patience. Your babies Chayson and Chasity are my babies. Thanks for loving and caring for me unconditionally.

To Angie Stone: as former label mates at a place that wasn't always pleasant, I admire you. You're the reason why I write songs.

To Felicia Papafio and Hannah: thanks for being there.

I want to thank all the DJs who took the science to unforgettable levels. Here's a list of a *few* of my friends: The Grand Wizard Theodore, my first student. Kool Herc. Pete DJ Jones. The supertechnical Grandmixer DT, who has always been ahead of his time. DJ Reggie Wells, for allowing me to get on the set at Club 371 in the Bronx. DJ Hollywood and LuvBug Starski, who can spin-rap-dance in just one show, also firsts. DJ Junebug, for giving a brother a break. African Islam, and Jazzy Jay, as well as Disco King Mario, for doing it on the East Side. Cut Creator. Terminator X. The Philly guys, Cash Money and Jazzy Jeff, who took the science to another level, as well as Joe Coolie, who took it higher out west. The one and only Jam Master Jay, R.I.P. Funkmaster Flex, amazing DJ, incredible entrepreneur. Dr. Premier, Imperial JC, DJ Breakout, A Trak, Qbert, Lil Louie

Vega—who's been a pure genius for so many, many years. Paul Oaken-fold—who's so hot but so cool, DJ Envy, DJ Enuff, DJ Coco Chenelle, DJ Plasticman, The Executioners, DJ JC in Atlanta, DJ Drama, DJ Irie, DJ Khaled, DJ Joe Koolie, DJ Dexter (Australia), DJ Mr. Cee, Francois K—whose musical voyage is astounding. Eric Morillo—Mister Excitement on the house tip. DJ Krush, for bringing my science to Japan; Fatboy Slim, for rocking my science in the UK; Kool DJ Red Alert; Chuck Chillout. Every mix show DJ. Every club DJ. Every street DJ and every other turntablist around the world who keeps the spirit of DJing alive, thriving, rocketing to new dimensions.

Finally, if I've left anyone off this list, owe it to my head and not my heart—you know I got mad love for you anyway.

David Ritz acknowledges:

Geoff Martin, the third author of this book, whose beautiful creative skills were instrumental in sculpting the story.

Grandmaster Flash, for whom I have great love and respect.

Janet Hill Talbert, who brought this book to life.

David Vigliano, Mike Harriot, Kirby Kim, faithful agents and friends.

My faithful family: Roberta, my soul mate, girlfriend, and wife; my daughters, Alison and Jessica; my sons-in-love, Jim and Henry; my grand-children, Charlotte Pearl, Alden, and James; my wonderful sisters, Eliza-beth and Esther; my loving nieces and nephews.

My loving friends Alan Eisenstock, Harry Weinger, Richard Freed, Rich-ard Cohen, Leo Sacks.

My fellowship brothers and sisters whom I've been blessed to meet on the road of happy destiny.

The spirit of the living Christ, the source of all love, the healer, and the hope.

Index

About the Authors

Joseph Saddler (Grandmaster Flash), a 2007 Rock and Roll Hall of Fame Inductee, is the celebrated pioneer of hip hop DJing, cutting, and sound mixing. Grandmaster Flash and the Furious Five fomented the musical revolution known as hip hop and were responsible for such masterpieces as "The Message" and "Grandmaster Flash on the Wheels of Steel." The combination of Grandmaster Flash's turntable mastery and the Furious Five's raps, which ranged from socially conscious to frivolously fun, made for a series of 12-inch records that forever altered the musical landscape. Saddler hosts a weekly Sirius Satellite Radio show, *DJ Grandmaster Flash*, on Hot Jamz (channel 50), Saturdays, 5–8 P.M. ET.

David Ritz (collaborator) is the critically acclaimed author of the bestselling biography *Divided Soul: The Life of Marvin Gaye* and coauthor of autobiographies of Smokey Robinson, Etta James, B.B. King, and Ray Charles. His book *Rhythm and the Blues*, cowritten with Jerry Wexler, won the 1993 Ralph J. Gleason First Prize for Best Music Book of the Year. David has written several novels, including *Blue Notes Under a Green Felt Hat*, and song lyrics, including those to "Sexual Healing." In 1992 he won a Grammy for liner notes he contributed to an album by Aretha Franklin.